中国思想文化术语多语种对外翻译
标准化建设项目成果
CHINESE THINKING AND CULTURE
MULTILINGUAL TERMINOLOGY DATABASE

中华源·河南故事
CHINESE CIVILIZATION
Stories from Henan

大运河
THE GRAND CANAL

主编 王清义
EDITOR-IN-CHIEF: WANG QINGYI

河南大学出版社
HENAN UNIVERSITY PRESS
·郑州·

图书在版编目（CIP）数据

中华源·河南故事．大运河：汉英对照 / 王清义主编． -- 郑州：河南大学出版社，2021.4
　ISBN 978-7-5649-4547-3

Ⅰ．①中… Ⅱ．①王… Ⅲ．①地方文化-河南-通俗读物-汉、英②大运河-文化史-河南-通俗读物-汉、英 Ⅳ．① G127.61-49 ② H12-49

中国版本图书馆 CIP 数据核字（2021）第 023681 号

责任编辑	谌洪波　张雪彩
责任校对	林方丽
封面设计	翟淼淼
出版发行	河南大学出版社
	地址：郑州市郑东新区商务外环中华大厦2401号　邮编：450046
	电话：0371-86059701（营销部）
	0371-86059750（高等教育与职业教育分公司）
	网址：hupress.henu.edu.cn
排　版	河南大学出版社设计排版部
印　刷	河南博雅彩印有限公司
版　次	2021年4月第1版　　印　次　2021年4月第1次印刷
开　本	710 mm×1010 mm　1/16　印　张　8.25
字　数	132千　　　　　　　　　定　价　42.00元

版权所有，侵权必究
本书如有印装质量问题，请与河南大学出版社营销部联系调换。

"中华源·河南故事"系列丛书编委会

顾　　问	黄友义　杨　平　范大祺
名誉主任	穆为民　何金平　刘炯天
主　　任	付　静
副 主 任	陈　岩　陈志伟　刁玉华　方启雄　介晓磊
	孔留安　李冰冰　李向前　李　镇　梁留科
	刘金锋　牛卫国　屈鹏飞　史永庆　田　凯
	万正峰　王建修　王清义　王自文　许二平
	杨建伟　杨玮斌　张改平　张俊峰　张明超
	张松文　赵卫东

主　　编	付静
副 主 编	李冰冰
编　　委	陈　玮　丁　锐　高　阳　徐恒振　郑延保

中华源·河南故事·大运河

主　　编	王清义
副 主 编	贾兵强　党兰玲（英文）
中文撰稿	贾兵强　陈　超
英文翻译	韩孟奇　刘全勇　雷冬雪
英文校对	〔美〕Cody Turner

The Editorial Committee
Chinese Civilization Stories from Henan

Consultants	Huang Youyi　Yang Ping　Fan Daqi
Honorary Directors	Mu Weimin　He Jinping　Liu Jiongtian
Director	Fu Jing
Deputy Directors	Chen Yan　Chen Zhiwei　Diao Yuhua　Fang Qixiong Jie Xiaolei　Kong Liu'an　Li Bingbing　Li Xiangqian Li Zhen　Liang Liuke　Liu Jinfeng　Niu Weiguo Qu Pengfei　Shi Yongqing　Tian Kai　Wan Zhengfeng Wang Jianxiu　Wang Qingyi　Wang Ziwen　Xu Erping Yang Jianwei　Yang Weibin　Zhang Gaiping Zhang Junfeng　Zhang Mingchao　Zhang Songwen Zhao Weidong
Chief Editor	Fu Jing
Deputy Chief Editor	Li Bingbing
Editors	Chen Wei　Ding Rui　Gao Yang　Xu Hengzhen Zheng Yanbao

Chinese Civilization Stories from Henan
The Grand Canal

Editor-in-Chief	Wang Qingyi
Associate Editors-in-Chief	Jia Bingqiang　Dang Lanling(English Text)
Writers	Jia Bingqiang　Chen Chao
Translators	Han Mengqi　Liu Quanyong　Lei Dongxue
Translation Proofreader	Cody Turner (U. S.)

总　序

　　中国是世界四大文明古国之一，也是世界上唯一的古代文明传统未曾中断的国家。河南省地处中国中东部，是中华文明和中华民族的重要发祥地，在中国五千年的文明史上，河南作为国家政治、经济、文化的中心就长达三千多年。从某种意义上讲，一部河南史就是半部中国史。这里是中华人文始祖黄帝的故乡，是古丝绸之路的东方起点，是少林功夫和陈氏太极的发源地，这里创建了中国历史上最早的都城，镌刻了中国最古老的文字，诞生了中国最初的商业文明。

　　伴随着新时代的荣光，河南经济社会发展迅速，人民生活水平显著提升，这是河南人民自力更生、艰苦奋斗的历史结果，也是对外开放带来的益处。河南经济社会的发展、人民生活方式的改变都植根于深层次的文化积淀。为了让世界更多地了解河南，让河南更好地走向世界，2018年以来，河南省人民政府外事办公室认真研析了这片古老土地上的历史文化资源和时代风貌，组织各领域权威专家学者，编译了"中华源·河南故事"中外文系列丛书，选取黄河文化、河洛文化、老子、庄子、黄帝、少林功夫、太极拳、中医、汉字、丝绸之路、古都、农业、大运河、文物、陶瓷、青铜器、手工艺、书法、杂技、豫菜、豫剧、脱贫攻坚、空中丝绸之路、航空城、南水北调、中国粮谷、红旗渠、焦裕禄等多个主题，力图以故事的方式向世界展现一个立体、全面、真实的河南。

　　当今世界，人类文明无论是在物质还是在精神方面都取得了巨大进步，特别是物质的极大丰富，这在古代世界是完全不能想象的。同时，当代人类也面临着许多突出的难题，比如，贫富差距持续扩大，物欲追求奢华无度，个人主义恶性膨胀，社会诚信不断消减，伦理道德每况愈下，人与自然关系日趋紧张，等等。要解决这些难题，不仅需要运用人类今天的智慧和力量，而且需要运用人类历史上积累和储存的智慧和力量。河南历史文化底蕴深厚、包容性强，在今天仍极具现实意义。中原文化蕴含的思想智慧有助于修身养性，推动人类社会进步发展，焦裕禄精神、红旗渠精神所体现的为民爱民、艰苦奋斗的价值取向是构建人类命运共同体的力量源泉。我们期待与读者们一起从河南故事中汲取更多的智慧和力量，共同创造更加美好的未来。

Series Foreword

China is one of the four ancient civilizations in the world, and is also the only country in the world where the ancient civilization has not been interrupted. Located in east-central China, Henan Province is an important cradle for the Chinese nation and Chinese civilization. In the course of the five thousand years of Chinese history, for more than three thousand years it served as the political, economic and cultural center of the country and therefore, as generally accepted, represents half of the history of China. Henan is the native place of Yellow Emperor, the cradle of Chinese culture, the starting point of the ancient Silk Road in the east, and the birthplace of Shaolin Kungfu and Chen-style Taijiquan—typical examples of the world-renowned Chinese martial arts. It was here that the earliest capital city in China was founded, the oldest Chinese characters engraved, and the earliest commerce took shape.

In the new era, Henan has witnessed rapid growth in its economy and remarkable improvement of people's living conditions owing to the national reform and opening-up policy and unremitting endeavors of the people. Modern economic achievements and social development as well as the changes of way of life could be traced back to its traditional values and cultural heritages. To enable people from other countries to understand Henan, and let the Province integrate more efficiently into the world development, the Foreign Affairs Office of the People's Government of Henan Province has organized teams of authoritative experts and scholars in relevant fields to compile this *Chinese Civilization: Stories from Henan* in Chinese and foreign languages since 2018 by crystallizing the excellence of traditions and outstanding features of modern development. The book series include *The Yellow River Culture*, *Heluo Culture*, *Laozi*, *Zhuangzi*, *The Yellow Emperor*, *Shaolin Kungfu*, *Taijiquan*, *Traditional Chinese Medicine*,

Chinese Characters, *The Silk Road*, *Ancient Chinese Capitals*, *Feeding the People—Agriculture*, *The Grand Canal*, *Cultural Heritage*, *Ceramic*, *Bronze*, *Handicraft Art*, *Calligraphy*, *Acrobatics*, *Henan Cuisine*, *Henan Opera*, *Poverty Alleviation*, *Silk Road in the Air*, *Zhengzhou—An Aviation City*, *South-to-North Water Diversion*, *China Grain Valley*, *Man-Made River—Hongqiqu Canal*, *A Model Official—Jiao Yulu*, etc., presenting a panoramic picture of the Province.

In today's world, human civilization has made great progress in both material accumulation and ethical advancement, and the great abundance of materials today, especially, is beyond the imagination of the ancient people. At the same time, however, modern people are also confronted with a lot of problems, such as the widening gap between the rich and the poor, the indulgence in pursuit of luxury and extravagance, the undesirable extension of individualism, the decline of social integrity, and the increasingly tense relationship between man and nature. To solve the problems, we need to draw on the wisdom and powers developed today as well as those accumulated in the past. Henan is endowed with rich historical and cultural heritages characterized by its inclusiveness, and such heritages remain significant today. The intelligence and wisdom in Henan culture are conducive to self-cultivation and to the promotion of social development. The spirit of serving the people and relentless struggle, as embodied in Jiao Yulu and Man-Made River—Hongqiqu Canal provides source of strength for building a community with a shared future for mankind. It is our hope that wisdom and strength from Henan stories could lead us to a shared brilliant future.

前　言

　　运河，是人类为着自身的生存和发展，以改造自然的智慧和力量开凿而成的人工河流。运河的开通，弥补了大自然的缺陷，发挥了运兵、运粮、运货、运客的重要功能。在人类文明的发展进程中，世界上的不少民族都曾开凿过一些运河，其中如沟通地中海与红海的苏伊士运河、贯通大西洋与太平洋的巴拿马运河，都是举世瞩目的浩大工程。然而，没有任何一条运河堪与中国的大运河相媲美。贯通中国南北的大运河，无论是开通时间之早，还是流经距离之长，均创下了世界之最的伟大纪录。

　　在开凿和修建中国大运河的过程中，春秋时期的吴王夫差、西汉时期的吴王刘濞、隋炀帝杨广、元代的郭守敬、明代的宋礼等一大批杰出的人物，充分施展自己的聪明才智，因地制宜，巧妙构思，精心设计，为大运河的建设做出了不可磨灭的贡献。中国大运河，以其历久不衰的顽强生命力，向世人充分地展示了中华民族丰富的想象力和创造力。

　　大运河与万里长城交相辉映，同为中华民族精神的标识。大运河由京杭大运河、隋唐大运河、浙东运河三部分构成，全长将近3200公里，是中国古代沟通南北交通的大动脉，也是世界上开凿最早、规模最大的运河，在人类文明中占有重要地位。

　　中国最早的运河来源于大禹治水的传说故事。但是直到隋代之前，原先在春秋时期修建的邗沟、战国时期魏国修建的鸿沟、三国时期曹魏修建的白沟、平虏渠、利漕渠以及吴国的破冈渎等运河规模都不大，而且相互之间不连贯，没有形成一个完整的水运系统。

到了隋朝统一全国后，隋炀帝杨广先后在605年、608年、610年征发百万民工修造了通济渠，改造了邗沟，又开凿了永济渠，重修江南河，从而形成了以洛阳为中心、北到河北涿郡、南达浙江余杭的中国历史上第一条贯穿国家南北的完整运河体系，这对于当时的经济发展、文化交流、国家统一和中央集权制的加强，都起到了重要作用。唐代则完全继承了隋代大运河体系，开创了大唐盛世。

北宋时期，中央政府也十分重视运河的作用。宋人先后开凿了汴河、惠民河、广济河、金水河等重要运河河道，把南、北方再次连接起来，从而保证了国家稳定和社会经济发展，进而开创了"东京梦华"的盛世景象。

到了元代，当时的元王朝又将大运河改弯取直，让江南的财富可以直接通过运河运送到北京，而不用再绕道洛阳。这奠定了京杭大运河的基本走向。

在中国大运河所流经的8个省份中，河南是最为核心的区域。这里不仅有大运河的遗脉，有安阳、洛阳、郑州、开封等4座古都，也有洛阳龙门石窟、安阳殷墟、登封"天地之中"历史建筑群、大运河、丝绸之路等5处世界文化遗产，更有洛阳隋唐大运河博物馆、朱仙镇木版年画、荥阳故城、商丘火神台庙会、河图洛书、巩义洛口仓、楚河汉界以及洛阳水席、郑州烩面、道口烧鸡等活化的运河文脉。而这些正是老家河南的名片，是河南故事的重要载体。

Preface

Canals, man-made waterways for human survival and development, usually play an important role in transporting troops, grain, passengers, etc. In the history of civilization, canals were built in many countries. Among them, the Suez Canal, connecting the Mediterranean Sea with the Red Sea, and the Panama Canal, linking the Atlantic Ocean and the Pacific Ocean, are great projects which attract worldwide attention. However, China's Grand Canal is second to none. Running through the north and south of China, it set the world's greatest record in terms of construction time and length.

During the period of its construction, numerous Chinese craftsmen and statesmen devoted large amount of hard work, among whom emerged a large number of outstanding people, such as Fuchai, the King of the State of Wu in the Spring and Autumn Period (770-476 BC), Liu Bi, the King of the State of Wu in the Western Han Dynasty, Emperor Yang (personal name Yang Guang) of the Sui Dynasty (581-618 AD), Guo Shoujing, a scientist in the Yuan Dynasty (1271-1368 AD), and Song Li, a government official in the Ming Dynasty (1368-1644 AD). All of them made great contributions to the Canal by giving full play to their own intelligence. After more than a thousand years, the Grand Canal, which is still running, has fully demonstrated rich imagination and creativity of Chinese people to the world with its enduring vitality.

Like the Great Wall, the Grand Canal is also a symbol of Chinese national spirit. Composed of the Beijing-Hangzhou Grand Canal, the Sui-Tang Grand Canal and the Zhedong Canal, with a total length of nearly 3,200 kilometers, it was the main artery of transportation between the north and the south in ancient China, and the earliest and longest canal in the world, occupying an important position in the history of human civilization.

The earliest canal in China originated from the legend of how Yu the Great controlled the floods. However, until the Sui Dynasty, a complete water transport system had not been established because the Hangou Channel originally built in the Spring and Autumn Period, the Honggou Channel built by the Wei State in the Warring States Period, the Baigou, Pinglu and Licao Channels by the Wei State and the Pogangdu Channel by the Wu State in the Three Kingdoms Period were not long enough and not connected with each other. Thus, a complete water transport system was not set up.

After unification of the whole country in the Sui Dynasty, Emperor Yang Guang (or Sui Yangdi) of the Sui Dynasty, recruited one million peasant laborers in the year of 605, 608 and 610 to build Tongji Channel, rebuild Hangou, dig Yongji Channel and rebuild Jiangnan River. As a result, a complete canal system, with Luoyang as the center, was set up, running from Zhuojun in Hebei Province in the north to Yuhang in Zhejiang Province in the south, which was the first canal across the north and south of the country in Chinese history. It played an important role in economic development, cultural exchanges, national unification and the strengthening of centralized systems at that time. The Grand Canal system of the Sui Dynasty was completely adopted by the Tang Dynasty and a prosperous era appeared.

In the Northern Song Dynasty (960-1127 AD), the central government also attached great importance to the Canal. People in the Song Dynasty successively dug main canals, such as Bianhe River, Huimin River, Guangji River and Jinshui River, which connected the north and the south again, thus ensuring national stability and socio-economic development, and then a prosperous age began in the Northern Song Dynasty.

In the Yuan Dynasty, the Grand Canal was straightened. The cargos from Jiangnan (south of the Yangtze River) were transported through the Canal directly to Beijing, bypassing Luoyang. So, the route of the Beijing-Hangzhou Grand Canal was opened.

Among the eight provinces that the Grand Canal flows through, Henan Province is in the middle section of the route. Here, people can not only visit the four ancient capitals, Anyang, Luoyang, Zhengzhou and Kaifeng, but also five world cultural heritages, including Luoyang Longmen Grottoes, Anyang Yin Ruins, Dengfeng Heaven and Earth Historical Building Complex, the Grand

Canal and the Silk Road. In addition, tourists can visit Luoyang Sui-Tang Grand Canal Museum, Xingyang Ancient Town, Shangqiu Huoshentai Temple Fair, Luokou Granary in Gongyi, and Chuhe Hanjie (literally the separating river of Chu and the boundary line of Han). Moreover, you can spend some time with Woodcut New Year Pictures of Zhuxianzhen, Hetu and Luoshu (mystic signs and markings revealed to Fu Xi and Yu the Great thousands of years ago, the preliminary record of the universal life rules). Finally, you can have a taste of local delicious foods, such as Luoyang Water Banquet Delicacies, Zhengzhou Stewed Noodles, Daokou Roast Chicken. All of the above are the name cards of Henan, and the carriers of Henan stories.

目 录　　　　　　　　　　　　　　　　Contents

第一章　运河发展史　　　　　　　　　　　001
　　一、大禹治水　　　　　　　　　　　　002
　　二、鸿沟开挖　　　　　　　　　　　　006
　　三、隋唐大运河　　　　　　　　　　　014

Chapter 1　The Development History of Canals　　001
　　Ⅰ. How Yu the Great Controlled Floods　　003
　　Ⅱ. The Construction of the Honggou Canal　　007
　　Ⅲ. The Sui-Tang Grand Canal　　015

第二章　运河功能价值　　　　　　　　　027
　　一、漕运之河　　　　　　　　　　　　028
　　二、运河的历史价值　　　　　　　　　040
　　三、运河的精神价值　　　　　　　　　046
　　四、运河的时代价值　　　　　　　　　052

Chapter 2　The Function of the Canal　　　027
　　Ⅰ. The River of Grain Transport　　　029
　　Ⅱ. The Historical Significance of the Canal　　041
　　Ⅲ. The Spiritual Significance of the Canal　　047
　　Ⅳ. The Epochal Significance of the Canal　　053

第三章　运河文化形态　　　　　　　　　057
　　一、运河古都　　　　　　　　　　　　058
　　二、运河城镇　　　　　　　　　　　　074
　　三、运河文脉　　　　　　　　　　　　092

Chapter 3　The Cultural Forms of the Canal	057
Ⅰ. The Ancient Capitals along the Canal	059
Ⅱ. The Towns along the Canal	075
Ⅲ. The Grand Canal Culture	093 |//
结语：走向世界的大运河	110
Summary: The Grand Canal—Open to the World	111 |//
附录：中国历史年代简表	114
Appendix: A Brief Chronology of Chinese History	114

第一章

运河发展史

Chapter 1

The Development History of Canals

一般来讲，运河就是与自然水道、沟渠河湖相连的人工水利设施。它具有航运、灌溉、分洪、运输的功能。中国的运河文化起源于河南，而中国最早的运河也是在河南境内修建的。中国最早的运河据说就是大禹当年带领百姓修建的。据记载，夏代运河就叫"大运河"。

一、大禹治水

洪水泛滥，当时治水能手大禹的父亲鲧，运用堵的方法，治水失败。大禹继承父亲遗志，认真总结经验，采取疏导的办法，带领人民治水。大禹翻山越岭，蹚河过川，用自己身体的长度作为标准，制造出了统一的测量工具，用规画圆，用矩做方，用准定平，用绳量长短。大禹从西向东，一路测度地形的高低，树立标杆，规划水道。根据水往低处流的特性，大禹改用疏导的办法治理洪水，故说"禹疏九河"，疏通了很多河道，让洪水通过河道，最后流到大海里去。就这样，经过了13年的励精图治，大禹历经千辛万苦，最终消除了洪水泛滥的灾祸。洪水终于退了，毒蛇猛兽被驱赶走了，人们把家搬了回来。大家在被水淹过的土地上耕种，农业生产渐渐恢复了，百姓重新过上了安居乐业的生活。大禹依靠疏导和筑堤堵水两个方法的结合制服了洪水，人们拥戴治水有功的大禹做了部落联盟的首领。

在治水的过程中，大禹对当地的地形情况非常熟悉，重新将天下划为"九州"，也就是冀州、徐州、兖州、青州、扬州、荆州、梁州、雍州和豫州。这也形成了中国最早的版图。所以，我们常将中国称为九州大地。通过治水，各部族之间的融合与合并不断加强，地域范围上有了空前的扩大，各部族间的协调和合作进一步加深，这就使得中原地区初步形成了以华夏族为中心，包括周围其他各族的一个很大的部族联合体。

大禹治水范围北到冀州部分地区，东到大海包括青、徐等州，东南及扬州，南达荆州北部，西到豫州、雍州部分地区，但治水核心区域是

Generally speaking, canals are man-made rivers connected with natural watercourses, ditches, lakes and rivers, which have functions in shipping, irrigation, flood diversion and transportation. Chinese canal culture originated in Henan Province, where the earliest canal in China was built. It is said that the earliest canal in China was built under the leadership of Yu the Great. Historical record had it that canal in the Xia Dynasty was called the Grand Canal.

Ⅰ. How Yu the Great Controlled Floods

In ancient China, floods regularly went rampant. Gun, Yu's father, tried to tame the water by blocking it, but ended in failure. Learning from his father's mistakes, Yu (or Dayu, with Da meaning great) inherited his father's will and led people to dredge river channels. Taking the length of his body as a standard, he invented unified measuring tools. The gauge was used to draw circle, rule for square, level for horizontal and rope for measuring. Travelling from the west to the east by crossing many mountains and rivers, Yu devoted himself to gauging the height of the terrains, setting benchmarks and planning waterways. Finally, he summed up a way to control floods—dredging waterways to clear obstacles for water flowing by making use of the downward flowing nature of water. A Chinese legend has it that Dayu dredged nine rivers, which means that he dredged many river channels and cleared obstacles, and finally brought floods to pass though planned waterways and into the sea. After 13 years of painstaking efforts, Yu brought floods under control at last. When floods receded and dangerous beasts and snakes were driven away, people moved back to their villages. They began to farm on the once flooded land and regained the life in peace and contentment. By both of dredging waterway and building dikes, Yu achieved a success in flood control, and eventually was elected as the leader of the tribal alliance.

During flood control, Yu got remarkably familiar with the local topography and landform. Hence, he divided the country into 9 states, namely Jizhou, Xuzhou, Yanzhou, Qingzhou, Yangzhou, Jingzhou, Liangzhou, Yongzhou and Yuzhou, which were the earliest layout of ancient China. Thanks to the early division, China is also called the land of 9 states. Yu's work also strengthened integration of different tribes, and enlarged the territory unprecedentedly. As a

黄河下游河道，还包括附近的河流、湖泊和沼泽。大禹治水开凿疏浚洪水的众多河渠通道中，最著名的是对黄河在平原南流的河道，文献称之为"鸿水"者，进行人工改造，以后多次改造后称之为鸿沟。鸿沟就是中国最早的运河水系，这是中国人开凿运河的开始。

　　大禹治水，一方面，打破了氏族间原有的界线，为新的行政建制的诞生创造了条件；另一方面，在治水过程中，必须依靠氏族联盟共同进行治水，由此促进了以血缘关系为纽带的氏族部落的大联合，促进了华夏各部族的融合与发展。大禹治水成功后，把组织严密、高度集权的治水机构逐渐沿袭为国家的组织机构，为国家的建立奠定了组织基础。由此，大禹治水催生了我国第一个奴隶制国家，人类社会进入文明时代。

大禹治水
Yu the Great fighting against the floods

result, a large tribal consortium was formed on the Central Plains with Huaxia nationality as the center and other ethnic groups included.

Yu's flood control work extended to some areas of Jizhou in the north, to the sea in the east, including Qingzhou and Xuzhou, Yangzhou in the southeast, northern Jingzhou in the south, and parts of Yuzhou and Yongzhou in the west. However, the core area was the lower reaches of the Yellow River, including nearby rivers, lakes and swamps. Among many river channels that Yu dredged, the most famous one was the channel of the Yellow River on the plains flowing to the south, which was called Hongshui in historical literatures. After many times of reconstruction, it was later called Honggou Canal which was the earliest canal system in China, and also the beginning of canal building in China.

By controlling floods, Yu broke the original boundary between the clans, making it possible to create a new administration system. Moreover, he promoted the great union and integration of tribes with blood relationship since joint efforts were needed to tackle water troubles. After the success in water control, the well-organized and highly-centralized water control institutions gradually evolved into a state organization, laying a foundation for the establishment of the country. It can be said that Yu's efforts in flood control, on the other hand, expedited the birth of the first state adopting slavery system in China, which also brought human society into an age of civilization.

二、鸿沟开挖

一提到古代运河，我们常认为公元前486年吴王夫差开凿的邗沟，是中国最早的运河。其实，鸿沟的开挖时间比邗沟还要早。周定王五年（前602年）以前，古之鸿沟（当时叫浪荡渠）就已建成并投入使用。此后，邗沟、郑国渠、灵渠等古代运河先后开挖修建。其中，鸿沟是中国古代最早沟通黄河和淮河的人工运河，这就是世界文化遗产之一——中国大运河通济渠的前身。

后来，魏惠王十年（前360年），由于战争需要，鸿沟重新开挖，位于古代荥阳成皋一带（今河南省郑州市荥阳）。魏惠王在位51年，见证了魏国由盛而衰的过程。在魏国国力强盛时期，魏惠王由安邑（今山西夏县）迁都大梁（今河南开封），魏国又称梁国，魏惠王也叫梁惠王。

魏惠王开凿鸿沟，虽然着眼于军事上和政治上的目的，在交通方面确实取得了一定的成就。但是，鸿沟最大的作用在于加强了魏国与其他地区的经济往来和文化交流。

鸿沟在经济方面的突出作用是促进了经济都会的兴起，最早受鸿沟影响而繁荣的是魏国的都城大梁（今河南开封）。魏公子信陵君有一次与魏王谈到魏国的河内、河外，即大梁附近的黄河以南与以北，"大县数百，名都数十"。由此可知，鸿沟带来了魏国的富庶以及大梁都会经济的繁荣。至于秦灭魏时，放黄河淹灌大梁，一是反映了大梁的富庶，民众兵悍，国力强固，使秦引之为惧，引之为恨；二是后人可由此知道历史上的大梁因得益于鸿沟而兴，因秦引黄河水灌城而遭毁灭。

大梁被淹而毁，但运河沿线的其他城市依然因得益于鸿沟而昌盛繁荣。荥阳因鸿沟的开凿而成为水道交通的要道。秦代用鸿沟漕运，在荥阳附近建敖仓，荥阳更加繁荣。睢阳因为城南的睢水和城北的获水与鸿沟通连，源源不断运来江淮间商品，而成为南北货物交换的繁华城市。

II. The Construction of the Honggou Canal

The mention of ancient canals in China often reminds people of the Hangou, or the Han Conduit, the earliest Chinese canal, constructed in 486 BC under the order of Fuchai, the King of the State of Wu, in the late Spring and Autumn Period (770-476 BC). As a matter of fact, Honggou, or the Hong Conduit, was even earlier. It had been completed and put into use before 602 BC, or the fifth year of the reign of King Ding of Zhou, the twenty-first King of the Zhou Dynasty, whose personal name was Ji Yu, while other ancient canals, like the Hangou, the Zhengguo Channel (or the Zhengguo Canal) and the Ling Channel (or the Lingqu Canal), were built later. As the earliest artificial waterway connecting the Yellow River and the Huaihe River, it is the precursor of the Tongji Channel (also Tongjiqu, or the Tongji Canal), one of the sections of the Grand Canal, a UNESCO World Cultural Heritage Site.

As historical records claim, the construction of Honggou Canal was initiated in the tenth year of the reign of King Hui of the State of Wei (360 BC) at the Chenggao area of the ancient Xingyang County (now a part of Xingyang City affiliated to Zhengzhou City of Henan Province) during the Warring States Period (475-221 BC). The fifty-one years of the reign of King Hui of Wei witnessed the ups and downs of the State. At the zenith of Wei's power, King Hui moved the capital from Anyi (now Xia County of Shanxi Province) to Daliang (now Kaifeng City of Henan Province), rendering another name to his State—Liang, and thus another title to himself—King Hui of Liang.

Although it was for the military and political ends that Honggou Canal was dug, it facilitated the civil transportation, and more importantly, enhanced the economic and cultural exchanges between Wei and other regions.

One of the prominent economic effects of Honggou was the rise of city economies. Daliang, the capital city, was a top exemplar of cities thriving on the convenience of Honggou. Prince Xinling, a prominent aristocrat, statesman and general of the State of Wei, once made references, in his conversation with the King of Wei, to the hundreds of large counties and dozens of famous cities located to the south and north of the Yellow River close to Daliang, reflecting

鸿沟
Honggou

还有陈（今河南淮阳），因为鸿沟的支流狼汤渠和颍水在此相会，而成为南北货物交流的码头和场所，并使陈国人沿习商贾职业。战国末年，楚国都城由郢都迁到陈，以陈作楚国都城，主要是因为陈的交通方便、商业繁荣。寿县（今安徽寿县）也是鸿沟系统中的一个都会，与寿县形成车辅之势的合肥等，皆因鸿沟的开凿而与中原连成一片，成为著名都会。鸿沟支流的下游与菏水下游相连，共同成就了彭城（今江苏徐州）。鸿沟上游与一些自然水道连通，而繁荣了其他运河城市，如山东临淄（今山东淄博）和河南洛阳。因由鸿沟西上西行的货物皆以洛阳为集散地，从而推动了洛阳城市经济的发展。此外，地处菏水、济水交汇点的陶（今山东定陶西北），也借鸿沟之利，成为交通方便的商业中心。

　　由于鸿沟水量充沛，与其相连的河道水位相对稳定，对发展航运很有利。鸿沟向南通淮河、邗沟与长江贯通；向东通济水、泗水，沿济水而下，可通淄济运河；向北通黄河，溯黄河西向，与洛河、渭水相连，使河南成为全国水路交通的核心地区。魏惠王所开凿的人工运河鸿沟，使开封城四周水道畅达，交通便利。今天，开封仍以多水而著称于世，

the considerable economic benefits brought by Honggou which nourished the richness of Wei and the prosperity of Daliang. Later, Qin, a powerful state, broke the bank of the Yellow River and annihilated Wei with flood. This could be a manifestation of two inferences: the prosperity and power of Wei which was so prominent that it even made Qin, the then strongest state, covetous and alarmed, and the role that water (like Honggou and the Yellow River) had played in the rise and fall of Daliang.

Despite the devastation of Daliang by flood, the other cities along Honggou prospered from it. Xingyang, for example, became one of the central hubs of the waterways. In the Qin Dynasty (221-206 BC), Honggou was used for the transport of grain, which led to the construction of Aocang, a great granary, near Xingyang. The granary brought more prosperity to Xingyang. Another example was Suiyang, a city with two streams connected to Honggou: the Sui River to the south and the Huo River to the north. Thanks to Honggou, the cargo going to and from between the Yangtze River and the Huaihe River turned Suiyang into a busy hub where goods from northern and southern China were gathered and exchanged. A similar success took place in Chen, now Huaiyang County of Henan Province. The crossing of the Langtang Canal, a branch of Honggou, and the Ying River here not only turned Chen into a busy dock and marketplace for goods from both the north and the south, but also formed a tradition of trade among the people of the State of Chen. In the ending years of the Warring States Period, the State of Chu moved its capital from Yingdu to Chen for, chiefly, its prosperity and its definite edge in transportation. Some cities of the Anhui Province, like Shouxian County and its interdependent neighbor Hefei, flourished for their close connections with the Central Plains since the completeness of Honggou. The connection of the lower stretch of the branch of Honggou with the lower stretch of the Heshui River, breathed life into the city of Pengcheng (now the Xuzhou City of Jiangsu Province). The connections of the upper stretch of Honggou with other natural waterways blessed nearby cities, like the Zibo City of Shandong Province, and the Luoyang City of Henan Province which served as a distributing center of goods transported upward and westward along Honggou, with booming economies. The city of Tao (now the northwest suburb of the Dingtao District of the Heze City of Shandong Province), thanks to its location

享有"北方水城"的美誉。

秦始皇统一中国后,充分利用了鸿沟水系和济水等河流,把在南方征集的大批粮食运往北方,并在鸿沟与黄河分流处兴建规模庞大的敖仓,作为转运站。秦末楚汉争霸即公元前206年夏,项羽带领楚军在彭城(今江苏徐州)战胜汉军,刘邦退到黄河南岸重镇荥阳。楚军乘胜追击汉军,在荥阳一带进行长达两年之久的战争,仍然不分胜负。公元前202年秋,楚军粮草耗尽,与汉军讲和。刘邦、项羽双方约定以鸿沟为界"中分天下",以西为汉,以东为楚。这就是历史上著名的"楚河汉界"典故。如今,中国象棋棋盘双方对垒的分界线就是以"楚河汉界"命名的。昔日"楚河汉界"的荥阳,正在结合楚汉文化、象棋文化,以鸿沟为中心,保护、挖掘、利用汉霸二王城的历史遗存与文化底蕴,着力建设世界象棋文化之都。

楚河汉界古战场风景区

"Chuhe Hanjie" ancient battlefield scenic spot

at the juncture of the Heshui River and the Jishui River, became a business center enjoying efficient transportation brought by Honggou.

The sustainable water flow of Honggou stabilized the levels of the waterways connected with it, thus made it ideal for transportation. To the south, it connected the Yangtze River via the Huaihe River and Hangou. To the east, it reached the Sishui River and had access to the Ziji Canal via the Jishui River. To the north, it led water into the Yellow River and further westward into the Luohe River and the Weishui River. With such an extensive network of water, Honggou turned Henan into a national hub of water transportation. This canal built under the order of King Hui of the State of Wei also wove Kaifeng City into the center of efficient waterways, which gained an honorable title of "Northern City upon Water".

After the unification of China by Qin Shi Huang, or the First Emperor of Qin in 221 BC, and the founding of the Qin Dynasty (221-206 BC), the water system of Honggou and streams like the Jishui River were efficiently used to transport grain collected from southern China to the north. Aocang, a large granary, was built where the Honggou joined the Yellow River as a forwarding station. Honggou became even more important politically in the following period historically called the Chu-Han Contention (206-202 BC) when Chu and Han, the two Powers that overthrew the Qin Dynasty, were competing for dominance. In the summer of 206 BC, the Chu armies led by Xiang Yu defeated Han in Pengcheng City (now Xuzhou City of Jiangsu Province), forcing Liu Bang, the leader of Han, into Xingyang, a town of military importance on the southern bank of the Yellow River. Chu attacked Xingyang incessantly in the following two years without gaining any success till the day when its provisions were exhausted. Left with no better choice, Chu and Han agreed to divide China into two parts with respective sovereignty divided by a median line, which was the Honggou, rendering the west to Han while the east, Chu. This famous treaty in Chinese history gave birth to an idiom—"Chuhe Hanjie", literally "the separating river of Chu and the boundary line of Han", symbolizing the border of two opposing Powers. These very Chinese characters of this idiom had been marked onto the board of the Chinese chess since then between the two frontlines, embodying the separating boundaries of the two opposing sides in the game, as you may still see

西汉时期,鸿沟被叫作狼汤渠。它北临万里黄河,西依邙山,东连大平原,南接中岳嵩山,是历代兵家兴师动众必争之地。800年后,隋炀帝以鸿沟为基础,修通大运河。此后百余年间,鸿沟漕运发达,成为交通要道。这就是中国大运河通济渠郑州段。元代建都北京,开京杭运河,水运干线东移,蔡河堵塞,鸿沟也就慢慢退出历史舞台。

隋唐大运河通济渠郑州段示意图
(来源:郑州市文物局)
Sketch map of Zhengzhou section of Tongji Channel of the Sui-Tang Grand Canal
(Source: Zhengzhou Cultural Heritage Administration)

today. At the historical site where these well-known events took place, Xingyang people are building their city into "A World Capital of Chinese Chess" by making full use of the culture of Chu and Han and Chinese chess, as well as the historical remains of the site.

During the period of the Western Han Dynasty (202 BC-9 AD), the Honggou was renamed the Langtang Channel. With the Yellow River stretching on the north, the massive Mangshan Mountain on the west, the vast plain on the east and Songshan Mountain, the central one of the Five Great Mountains of China on the south, the geographical location of the Honggou made itself a hotspot of war throughout the dynasties. Eight hundred years later, based on the Honggou, Emperor Yang of the Sui Dynasty (581-618 AD), who moved the capital from Daxing (now Xi'an) of Shaanxi Province to Luoyang of Henan Province, built the Grand Canal of Sui, the precursor and the major component of the Beijing-Hangzhou Grand Canal, connecting Luoyang with Hangzhou of Zhejiang Province. Since then, the Honggou became the Zhengzhou section of the Tongji Channel of the Grand Canal of Sui, serving as an important hub with its superiority in transportation throughout the following hundreds of years. In the Yuan Dynasty (1271-1368 AD) when Beijing was the capital, the route of the Canal was changed and the main sections moved eastward. As a result, the Caihe River was jammed, which led to the exit of Honggou from this stage of history.

三、隋唐大运河

　　隋唐大运河是中国大运河不可或缺的一部分，在中国运河史上具有不可替代的地位和作用。隋唐大运河以洛阳为中心，分为永济渠、通济渠、邗沟、江南河四段，沟通五大水系，穿越8省、市，全长2700公里，其开凿之早、规模之大、里程之长在我国交通史、政治史、文化史、经济史、社会史上均具有举足轻重的地位。

　　581年，隋朝建立，定都大兴城（今陕西西安）。589年，隋朝灭了南方的陈朝，结束了长达300多年的南北分裂局面，继秦朝后再一次统一了中国。隋朝立国之初，为了保证京师的供给，必须要将江淮地区的粮食物资运往京师，于是隋文帝下令修凿运河，开展漕运。

　　始建于汉武帝时期的漕渠在隋代被重新启用。漕渠自凿通之后700多年间，历经多次战乱，以致河道淤塞，难以行船。隋文帝要利用这条现成的运河，开水运直通南方，工程由营新都副监宇文恺负责。重新开挖的漕渠从大兴城开始直至潼关，全长400里。工程竣工后，这段漕渠被改名为"广通渠"。广通渠疏通后，比原来的陆路运输一年内可以节省上亿银两的运输费用。从此大兴城与潼关间的商业往来更加频繁，工商业得到了极大的发展。无论官府还是百姓，都对这条运河赞不绝口。

　　总指挥宇文恺在主持开凿广通渠时，不是简单地疏浚汉代漕渠的河床，而是在原有河床的基础上统一规划航道，还在航道上设立保证运河水位的一系列闸坝，使这条运河可以通行拥有四个桅杆、四张大帆的巨船。这条运河的凿通，为后来隋朝大运河的兴建积累了宝贵的技术经验。

　　当时南朝最后一个政权陈还未被彻底消灭，为了实现全国的完全统一，隋文帝准备大举伐陈。587年，隋文帝下诏开凿山阳渎。山阳渎北起山阳（今江苏淮安），南至邗城（今江苏扬州），基本上就是春秋时吴国邗沟的故道。重新开凿这条运河一方面是为了保障伐陈战争的补给，

III. The Sui-Tang Grand Canal

As an indispensable part of China's Grand Canal, the Sui-Tang Grand Canal played an irreplaceable role in the history of China's canals. Centered at Luoyang and with a length of 2,700 kilometers, the Sui-Tang Grand Canal was divided into four sections, i.e. Yongji Channel, Tongji Channel, Hangou and Jiangnan River, connecting five major water systems and crossing eight provinces and cities. It occupied an influential position in the history of China's transportation, politics, culture, economy and society so far as its construction time, scale and length are concerned.

In 581, the Sui Dynasty was established with Daxing (now Xi'an, Shaanxi Province) as its capital. In 589, the Sui Dynasty put an end to more than 300 years of division between the north and the south, and reunified China after the Qin Dynasty. At the beginning of the Sui Dynasty, in order to supply the capital, Emperor Wen ordered the construction of a canal so that grain from Jianghuai region could be carried to the capital by water.

隋文帝
Emperor Wen of the Sui Dynasty

宇文恺

Yuwen kai

另一方面也是为将来的漕运准备好水上通道。山阳渎开通后,隋文帝在运河沿岸设置了粮食储运基地。漕运的兴盛使大兴官仓内的粮食堆积如山,多达上千万石[1],布匹也有上千万匹之多。到了隋文帝末年,国家储备的物资可供50年之用,而大兴的库存直到唐朝又用了20年仍未用完。

605年,隋炀帝登上皇位,并迁都洛阳。洛阳地处中原,地理位置上具有驾驭全中国的气势,同时又因大兴城所处的关中平原狭小闭塞,当时已经难以负担对京师的供应,而迁都四通八达的洛阳正好符合当时

---

[1] "石"是古代的一种度量单位。隋唐时一石约为53.6千克,宋代一石约为59.2千克。

The channels built during the reign of Emperor Wudi of the Han Dynasty were reused in the Sui Dynasty. For more than 700 years since they were dug, these channels had been silted up due to frequent wars. Emperor Wen of the Sui Dynasty wanted to make use of these ready-made channels for water transport directly to the south of China. He ordered a government official Yuwen kai to be in charge of the reconstruction of the channels, ranging from Daxing to Tongguan with a length of 200 kilometers, which was renamed the Guangtong Channel after the completion. With the opening of the Guangtong Channel, hundreds of millions of silver dollars could be saved compared with land transport. From then on, the commercial exchanges between Daxing and Tongguan became more frequent and the economy fully developed. Both the government and the people spoke highly of the Guangtong Channel.

When the Guangtong Channel was dug under the command of Yuwen kai, instead of simply dredging the riverbed of the Han Dynasty canal, the course was planned on the basis of the old riverbed. Besides, a series of dams and sluice gates were built to maintain water level in the waterway so that large boats with four masts and four large sails could pass through. In a word, the construction of the Guangtong Channel offered wide experience for the Grand Canal of the Sui Dynasty.

One of the most important reasons for Emperor Wen to build the Canal was to reunify the whole China. At that time, he was prepared to launch a strong attack on Chen, the last regime in the Southern Dynasty. In 587, Emperor Wen ordered the construction of Shanyangdu Channel starting from Shanyang in the north (now Huai'an, Jiangsu Province) and ending in Hancheng (now Yangzhou, Jiangsu Province) in the south, which was the old course of the Hangou in the Spring and Autumn Period. The Channel was rebuilt not only for war supplies, but also for future water transport. After the completion of Shanyangdu Channel, Emperor Wen set up grain storage and transport bases along it. Thanks to the water transport, grain and cloth were piled up like mountains in the official storehouse of Daxing. By the end of Emperor Wen's reign, the reserve materials could be used for 50 years, and the materials stored in Daxing were not used up 20 years after the Tang Dynasty.

In 605, Emperor Yang ascended the throne and moved his capital to

的政治、经济发展趋势，更有利于稳定局势。继位之后，隋炀帝就准备以洛阳为中心开凿一条贯穿南北的大运河。

当年，隋炀帝征发百万民工，疏通济渠。因为大量使用古运河的现成河道，所以这条千里长河只用了155天即告竣工。通济渠河宽40步、水深4米，不仅在漕运方面起着重要作用，而且还具备引水、蓄水、分洪、灌溉、绿化和改良两岸土壤等功能。为了庆祝这条运河的通航，隋炀帝为之举行了极大规模的庆祝仪式。在向新渠引水的同时，隋炀帝又下诏建造龙舟，组成一支庞大的舰队。其中，最大的龙舟长二十丈[1]，宽三丈，高四丈五，船上有四层建筑，120个房间。最上一层造有三间大殿，殿上起楼，楼外有阁，处处雕栏彩绘，以珠玉和五彩锦幕装饰，整个大船就像一座水上皇宫。

通济渠通航的第二年即606年，由于漕运顺畅，漕粮被大量运至洛阳。为了储存这些粮食，隋炀帝下诏在洛阳以东的巩县（今河南巩义市东北）修筑洛口仓，并在粮仓外筑城以进行保护，同时挖了3000个地窖，每窖都可以储存8000石粮食。洛阳西北方又建了座方圆十里的回洛仓，这座仓城有地窖300个。洛阳城外的这两处大仓可储藏粮食2640万石，成为洛阳的主要供给保障。

608年，为了向北方用兵，隋炀帝又征集河北一带的民夫上百万人，开凿南起黄河、北至涿郡（今北京）的永济渠，全长2000余里。永济渠的开凿也利用了大量的天然河道和古运河。其南段河道是将黄河支流沁水的天然河道拓宽、疏浚、加深而成，下与通济渠相连。与通济渠的漕运用途不同，隋炀帝开凿永济渠主要是为军事服务的。611年，永济渠全线竣工。隋炀帝乘龙舟顺着永济渠北上巡视，从江都穿过淮河、黄河，进入永济渠，再经过海河，直达涿郡。巡游中，他还详细了解了当地的民情和北部边陲外少数民族政权的情况。

---

[1] "丈"是古代的一种度量单位。隋唐时一丈约为2.95米。

Luoyang, located in the Central Plains with convenient transportation. From geographical view, moving the capital was conducive to his rule and to the political and economic development of the whole country at that time. After he succeeded to the throne, Emperor Yang was going to build a canal running through the north and south of China with Luoyang as the center.

In the same year, Emperor Yang recruited one million of laborers to dredge the Tongji Channel. It took only 155 days to clear the river of over 500 kilometers because of the ready-made river courses of the ancient canals. The Tongji Channel was 40 steps wide and 4 meters deep. It not only played an important role in water transport, but also had the functions of water diversion, water storage, flood diversion, irrigation, greening and soil improvement on both sides of the river. To celebrate its navigation, Emperor Yang held a grand ceremony. While diverting water to the new canal, Emperor Yang ordered to build dragon boats to form a fleet, among which the largest dragon boat was 20 zhang [1] in length, 3 zhang in width and 4.5 zhang in height. It had four floors and 120 rooms. On the top floor, three main halls were built. On the top of the halls, there were buildings with pavilions outside. The largest dragon boat was like a palace on water with columns beautifully carved and the hull colorfully painted.

In 606, a large amount of grains were transported to Luoyang thanks to the smooth navigation of the Tongji Channel. In order to store these grains, Emperor Yang ordered Luokou Granary in Gongxian County (now northeast of Gongyi City), east of Luoyang, and a wall outside the granary for protection, to be built. At the same time, 3,000 cellars were dug, each of which could store 8,000 dan [2] of grain. In addition, the other granary called Huiluo was built in the northwest of Luoyang which had 300 cellars. With a store capacity of 26.4 million dan of grain, the two large granaries outside Luoyang became Luoyang's main food supply.

In 608, Emperor Yang, for military purpose in the north, recruited about one

---

[1] Zhang is a unit of length in ancient China. One zhang equals about 2.95 meters in Sui and Tang dynasties.

[2] Dan is a unit of weight in ancient China. One dan equals about 53.6 kilograms in Sui and Tang dynasties and 59.2 kilograms in the Song Dynasty.

隋炀帝
Emperor Yang of the Sui Dynasty

关于隋炀帝修大运河的原因,有很多种说法。广为流传的是,江苏扬州开了一种十分绮丽的花——琼花,隋炀帝听说后,就决定去赏花。于是他动用大量人力,开通了大运河,并乘豪华龙舟前往。可是,琼花讨厌这位暴虐的君主,他来时就自行败落,不让隋炀帝看。也相传隋炀帝为了下江南遍寻江南美女而开凿大运河。但隋炀帝下令修建大运河,当然不全是为了个人享乐和腐朽生活。通过研究隋朝大运河的路线,我们不难发现隋炀帝修建大运河的真正原因。隋朝大运河和后来的京杭大运河不同的是,隋朝大运河以洛阳为中心,呈一个倒"V"结构,换句话说,隋朝大运河并不是由起点直接通往作为终点的幽州,而是折转前往当时的首都洛阳,再从洛阳前往幽州。众所周知,南北朝长期分裂,虽然隋文帝时期实现了国家的统一,但是南北之间文化和经济上的差距,不利于南北经济交流和政权稳固。而修建大运河,以洛阳为中心,把江淮地区、关中地区和华北平原有机连在了一起。这样,一方面加强了南北政

million laborers from Hebei to dig the Yongji Channel from the Yellow River in the south to Zhuojun (now Beijing) in the north. Many natural river courses and ancient canals were integrated into the Yongji Channel with a total length of more than 1,000 kilometers. The south section of the Yongji Channel was built by widening, dredging and deepening the natural river course of Qinshui, a tributary of the Yellow River, and then connected with the Tongji Channel. Different from Tongji Channel's water transport purpose, Emperor Yang's Yongji Channel was mainly for military use. In 611, the entire Yongji Channel was completed. The Emperor toured north along the Yongji Channel by the dragon boat, crossing the Huaihe River and Yellow River from Jiangdu, entering Yongji Channel, passing the Haihe River and reaching Zhuojun (now Beijing). During the tour, he also learned in detail about the local people's lives and ethnic minority regimes outside the northern border.

Legends have it that there were many reasons why Emperor Yang built the Grand Canal. It is widely spread that a kind of beautiful flowers, called Qiong flower, grew in Yangzhou, Jiangsu Province. After learning this, he decided to go to see the flowers. So he recruited a large number of laborers to build the Grand Canal, and went there by a luxury dragon boat. However, Qiong flowers disliked the tyrannical Emperor and withered before he arrived there. It was also said the Emperor dug the Grand Canal in order to have fun with beautiful women in Jiangnan (south of the Yangtze River). However, the reason why Emperor Yang ordered the building of the Grand Canal was not all for personal enjoyment and extravagant life. By studying the route of the Grand Canal in the Sui Dynasty, we can easily find out the real reason. The difference between the Sui Dynasty Grand Canal and the Beijing-Hangzhou Grand Canal is that the former is shaped like an upside-down V with Luoyang at the top. In other words, the Grand Canal of the Sui Dynasty did not run directly from the starting point to Youzhou, the terminal, but turned to Luoyang, the capital at that time, and then went from Luoyang to Youzhou. It is well known that the Northern and Southern dynasties were divided for a long time. Although the whole country was unified by Emperor Wen of Sui, the cultural and economic gap between the north and the south became an obstacle to the economic exchange and political stability between the north and the south. The Grand Canal with Luoyang as the center connected

治上的联系，另一方面也可以借用南方的物资，支持中原地区的发展。而以板渚为转折点的北端，其作用其实就带有很大的军事意义。当然，在隋炀帝时期，一个非常重要的事件，便是隋炀帝对于东北地区高句丽的征服以及对于整个北方边防补给的考量。毕竟无论是对高句丽地区的控制，还是要在这一地区维持庞大的军队边防，单纯依靠北方边境地区为军队提供给养，显然无法自给自足，通过开通运河，便可以有效地为边境军队补充战略物资。

隋炀帝把大运河留给了大唐王朝。盛唐之盛，盛在运河；大唐之大，大在运河。站在盛唐中心的，不是帝王，不是贵妃，不是文武大臣，而是长安望春楼下自隋流来的大运河。唐代疏浚隋运河并开挖汴河，其连接黄河和淮河，西通河洛，南达江淮，成为唐代大运河的主要河段，形成了四通八达的水运网，并且唐代设置了专门官职管理河道事务，使其航运能力大大提高，对唐王朝的兴盛发挥了极大作用。唐诗中以大运河为审美对象的诗歌创作数量众多。如李敬方的《汴河直进船》，"汴水通淮利最多，生人为害亦相和。东南四十三州地，取尽脂膏是此河"，准确地反映出大运河成为维系唐王朝的生命线的事实。皮日休的《汴河怀古》，"尽道隋亡为此河，至今千里赖通波。若无水殿龙舟事，共禹论功不较多"，更是看到大运河作为水利工程造福后世的价值。可以说，隋唐大运河奠定了唐宋数百年间国家的长治久安、人民的安居乐业。

以洛阳为中心和枢纽的隋唐大运河成为中国古代特别是隋、唐、宋时期中国南北交通的大动脉。隋唐时期，关中地区"号称沃野，然其土地狭，所出不足以给京师"，这就需要从黄河下游、河北平原和江淮地区等物产丰富的地方调运粮食和其他物资。为配合漕运，隋唐时期在以洛阳为中心的运河沿线修建了洛口、黎阳、回洛等多个粮仓。其中，回洛仓仓城的仓窖数量多达700座左右。作为庞大农业帝国的生命线，隋唐大运河的年漕运能力曾多达七八百万石。

隋唐大运河不仅是首次贯通南北且规模空前的全国性运河体系，而

Jianghuai area, Guanzhong area and north China Plain. The navigation of the Canal strengthened the political ties between the north and the south; moreover, it could also help the development of the Central Plains with the materials from the south. Finally, the northern end of Banzhu was of great military significance. During Emperor Yang's reign, a very important event was his conquest of Koguryo in northeast China, and then the replenishment of the northern frontier was his concern. Thus, the construction of the Canal was a must for providing supplies and other strategic raw materials for the army.

The Grand Canal was Emperor Yang's heritage to the Tang Dynasty, which was a symbol of its power and prosperity. In the Tang Dynasty, the Sui Canal was dredged and the Bianhe River was built. The Grand Canal was connected with the Yellow River and Huaihe River. The main section of the Canal in the Tang Dynasty passed through Heluo in the west and reached Jianghuai in the south, forming a water transport network. Special official positions were set up to manage river affairs, and the shipping capacity was greatly improved. The Grand Canal played a great role in the prosperity of the Tang Dynasty. A few poets in the Tang Dynasty composed many poems for the Grand Canal, some of which reflected the fact that the Grand Canal became the lifeline of the Tang Dynasty, while others the value of the Grand Canal as a water conservancy project to benefit future generations. It can be said that the Sui-Tang Grand Canal laid the foundation for the long-term stability of the country and the content and peaceful life of the people during the Tang and Song dynasties.

The Sui-Tang Grand Canal running from the north to the south, with Luoyang as its center and hub, was a main artery in transportation in ancient China, especially in Sui, Tang and Song dynasties. During the Sui and Tang dynasties, the land in Guanzhong area (currently known as Guanzhong Plain in Shaanxi Province) was fertile but did not produce enough to meet the needs of the capital. Thus, it was necessary to transfer grain and other supplies from such abundant places as lower reaches of Yellow River, Hebei Plain and Yangtze-Huaihe Region. To facilitate transportation of grain by water, many granaries were built in Luokou, Liyang and Huiluo, etc. along the Canal. Among them, about 700 grain cellars were built in Huiluo Granary. As the lifeline for a large agricultural empire, the Grand Canal had an annual average transportation

且是服务于统一的中央政府的航运通道。与京杭大运河相比,隋唐大运河长度是京杭大运河的 1.5 倍。隋唐大运河更能代表鼎盛时期中华文明。隋唐大运河不仅为隋唐东都洛阳、北宋东京开封提供了强有力的物质保障和国家战略储备,辐射长安、洛阳、开封、杭州、扬州等世界级大城市,而且凸显了大运河的政治、经济、文化和军事功能,对进一步强化隋唐时期的国家统一、经济发展和文化兴盛发挥了重要作用;同时,为贞观之治、开元盛世等鼎盛局面的形成以及促进国家的繁荣富强奠定了重要基础。

在开凿和维护隋唐大运河的过程中,隋唐大运河河南段不仅开创了应对多种情况的治水理论和治水方略,而且最早成功运用闸、坝、堤、堰、弯道等建造技术,巧妙地解决了跨越黄河水系以及不同河流自然环境下的水源、泥沙和洪水等问题,为后来的京杭大运河的泥沙治理问题积累了经验。

capacity of 7 million dan to 8 million dan.

The Sui-Tang Grand Canal, 1.5 times as long as the Beijing-Hangzhou Grand Canal, was not only the first nationwide canal system running from the north to the south, but also the shipping channel of the central government. It is more representative as a symbol of Chinese civilization in its heyday. The Grand Canal provided Luoyang, the capital of Sui and Tang dynasties, and Kaifeng, the capital of the Northern Song Dynasty, with sufficient grain and other strategic reserves, having great effect on many other metropolises like Chang'an, Hangzhou, Yangzhou, etc. Therefore, it played a significant role in further strengthening the national unification and the development of economy and culture by its multiple functions. In addition, it laid a solid foundation for the country's prosperity and strength, especially in Excellent Governance during the Zhenguan Times (Emperor Li Shimin) and Kaiyuan Flourishing Age (Emperor Li Longji).

In the process of the building and maintenance of the Sui-Tang Grand Canal in Henan section, some effective strategies on water control were adopted. Pound locks, dams, embankments and weirs were built to solve the problems of crossing the Yellow River, water distribution, sediment, flooding in different rivers, and much experience was gained for the later sediment control of the Beijing-Hangzhou Grand Canal.

第二章
运河功能价值

Chapter 2

The Function of the Canal

水是生命的源泉。有了水，才有生命，才有生机勃勃的创造。而河流则是人类古代文明的摇篮。源源不断的河水给人们带来充足的水源，解决了生活和生产之需，也为人们的出行、交往提供了便利。

中国的悠久历史和灿烂文化，与江河密不可分。虽说在形成的历史和涵盖的区域上，大运河难以与黄河、长江相提并论，然而作为中国大地上唯一的纵贯南北的大河，大运河在沟通南北之间经济、文化的交流和促进政治统一方面所发挥的作用也是包括黄河、长江在内的任何一条自然河流所无法取代的。人们常把中国比喻为一条巨龙，而千里京杭大运河，便是这条巨龙搏动不息的主动脉。通过它，巨龙全面吸收各处的养分并输送到每个角落，使龙头至龙尾能够得到均衡的发展。可以说，如果没有这条龙脉，也就不会有古中国这条傲视世界的巨龙。

中国大运河是国家的大运之河，是漕运之河、航运之河，在维护国家统一、繁荣社会经济、推动民族融合、促进文化交流、兴盛沿线城市等方面发挥了重要的作用。大运河文化是实现国家认同的重要文化纽带，是中国精神的符号。中国特色社会主义进入新时代，传承与弘扬大运河文化，具有极大的时代价值和现实意义。

一、漕运之河

漕运发端于春秋战国，发展在秦汉，繁荣在隋唐。隋唐大运河首次将南北的天然河道与人工工程连接起来，促进了隋唐时期国家的统一与经济繁荣、文化交流，在大运河的发展史上具有里程碑的意义。自南宋以来，唐宋运河河南段渠道逐渐淤塞。到了元代，由于政治中心东移、北移，经济重心南移，为了便于南方粮食的运输，大运河被裁弯取直，形成了京杭大运河的规模。

隋炀帝开凿通济渠，联结河、淮、江三大水系，形成沟通南北的新的漕运通道，奠定了后世大运河的基础。开皇三年（583年），隋文帝

Water is the source of life. With water, there is life and creation. Rivers are the cradle of ancient civilization. The continuous flow of rivers brings people sufficient water, thus meeting the needs for life and production and providing convenience for people's travel and communication.

China's long history and splendid culture are interwoven with rivers. In history, the Grand Canal is hardly comparable with the Yellow River and the Yangtze River, but as the only great man-made watercourse that runs from the north to the south in China, the role that the Grand Canal has played in the economic and cultural exchanges between the north and the south and the promotion of political unity, cannot be replaced by any other natural river. If China is a dragon, the Grand Canal will be the dragon's main artery, through which the dragon fully absorbs nutrients and transports them to all parts of its body for its balanced development. It can be said that there would not have been so great a country in the world without such a river.

Besides its function as a grain shipment route and major vein of river-borne indigenous trade in China, the Grand Canal played an important role in maintaining national unification, promoting ethnic integration and cultural exchanges and boosting economy of the cities along the route. The Grand Canal culture, a symbol of Chinese spirit, is an important cultural tie to maintain national identity. Now China has entered a new era and it is of great significance to inherit and promote the Grand Canal culture.

Ⅰ. The River of Grain Transport

Canal transport originated in the Spring and Autumn Period and the Warring States Period, developed in the Qin and Han dynasties, and flourished in the Sui and Tang dynasties. The Sui-Tang Grand Canal, a milestone in the history of the Grand Canal, connected the natural rivers and artificial channels for the first time, which promoted the national unification, economic prosperity and cultural exchanges in the Sui and Tang dynasties. Since the Southern Song Dynasty, the Henan section of the Tang and Song Canal gradually silted up. In the Yuan Dynasty, with the political center moving eastward and northward, and the economic center southward, the Grand Canal was straightened to facilitate

曾先后在河南、陕西运渠所在沿岸广泛设置粮仓，并招募运丁，把河北、山西、山东等地的粮食都汇集到粮仓。隋灭了南陈后，大兴城的粮食大部分开始从江淮地区输送。唐代，中央政府通过对运河的疏浚，重新建立起了漕运仓储制度。

为了有力支持漕运，隋唐两代在运河沿线设置了很多大型的粮仓。例如，在隋炀帝大业初年（605～606年），新设置的回洛仓周长十几里，设有300多处大型窖藏。这之后回洛仓又经不断扩建。朝廷更是将周边老百姓和其他地方的富商大贾迁移到这里。根据近年来的考古发掘，回洛仓拥有仓窖700座左右，是目前国内考古发现仓窖数量最多的古代粮仓。入唐以后又增设了河阴等大型粮仓，其他还有几处规模较小的粮仓，建立起了一套完备的粮食储存体系，为社会发展奠定了良好的物质基础。

回洛仓遗址

Ancient site of Huiluo Granary

grain transportation in the south, which resulted in the Beijing-Hangzhou Grand Canal of today.

Emperor Yang of the Sui Dynasty ordered to dig the Tongji Channel to connect three river systems, namely the Yellow River, the Huaihe River and the Yangtze River, and a new canal transport channel to connect the north and the south was built, which laid the foundation for the later Grand Canal. For example, in the third year of Kaihuang (583 AD), Emperor Wen of the Sui Dynasty had extensively set up granaries along the banks of canals in Henan and Shaanxi. He also recruited laborers to collect the grain of Hebei, Shanxi, Shandong and other places into the granaries. After Sui replaced South Chen Dynasty (557-589 AD), most of Daxing's grain began to be transported from the Jianghuai region (areas along the Yangtze River and the Huaihe River). In the Tang Dynasty, the central government rebuilt the grain transport and storage system by dredging the canal.

In order to support the grain transport, many large granaries along the canal were set up in the Sui and Tang dynasties. For example, in the early years (605-606 AD) of Emperor Yang of the Sui Dynasty, the newly-set Huiluo Granary was more than 5 kilometers in circumference, with more than 300 large cellars. Since then, the Huiluo Granary was continuously expanded and the government moved people and wealthy merchants from other places to the area. According to the recent archaeological excavations, there were about 700 cellars in Huiluo Granary, which was the largest ancient granary in China found by domestic archaeology at present. In the Tang Dynasty, large granaries such as Heyin and several smaller granaries were built. Then, a complete set of grain storage system was set up, which laid a good foundation for social development.

During the Sui and Tang dynasties, the Yongji Channel on the Hebei Plain was the main watercourse to transport grain from Hebei and military grain to the north in times of war. At the same time, the Yongji Channel also undertook the important mission of transferring materials from the Jianghuai region to the north. Emperor Yang of the Sui Dynasty made full use of the Liyang Granary along the Yongji Channel to transport grain, grass and other supplies during his military expedition to the region in the east of the Liaohe River. In the archaeological excavation of the Liyang Granary, the remains of a canal about 8 meters wide were found in the north and central part of Cangcheng, which

在隋唐时期，河北平原上的永济渠是调运河北地区粮食的主要通道，也是对北方用兵时输送军粮的主要路线。同时，永济渠还承担着转运江淮地区物资北上的重要使命。隋炀帝征伐辽东时就充分利用了永济渠上的黎阳仓，调运粮草和物资。在对黎阳仓的考古发掘中，在仓城北中部就发现了宽约 8 米的漕渠遗存，形成了一个完整的粮仓与黄河、永济渠相互贯通的漕运水系。直至隋末，积储在涿郡的粮食仍十分丰富。唐代前期对辽东用兵过程中所使用的军粮绝大部分取自河南、河北二地。到了唐中期，通过改革漕运，每三年所运送的漕粮就多达 700 万石，效果十分显著。

江南河杭州段

The Hangzhou section of Jiangnan River

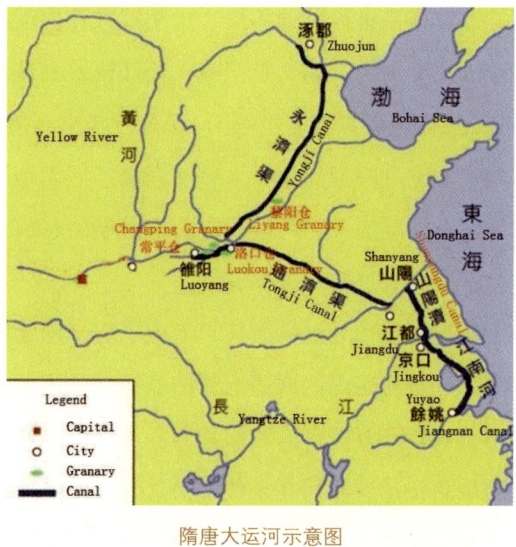

隋唐大运河示意图
(来源：国家文物局)
Sketch map of the Sui-Tang Grand Canal
(Source: National Cultural Heritage Administration)

formed a complete canal transport system connected with the Yellow River and the Yongji Channel. Until the end of the Sui Dynasty, the grain stored in Zhuojun was still abundant. In the early Tang Dynasty, most of the military supplies used in the military expedition to the region in the east of the Liaohe River were from Henan and Hebei Provinces. By the middle of the Tang Dynasty, through the reform of canal transport, 7 million dan of grain was transported every three years successfully.

In the Sui and Tang dynasties, the Tongji Channel, the Shanyang Channel (the Hangou Canal) and the Jiangnan River leading to the southeast were the main waterways for transporting food and materials in the Jianghuai region. According to the records, the grains collected from the lands in the Yangtze River Basin and the Pearl River Basin were transported to Yangzhou first, then to Luoyang by the Tongji Channel and other channels. Located on the bank of the Yongji Channel, Qinghe Commandery (now Qinghe County, Hebei Province) was called the North Granary in China. It was the place in which a large amount of cloth and grain collected from the Jianghuai and Henan regions

隋唐时期，通向东南地区的通济渠、山阳渎和江南河，是输送江淮地区粮食、物资的主要渠道。据文献记载，长江流域和珠江流域的租庸调都先运至扬州，再由通济等渠运至洛阳。地处永济渠一侧的清河郡（今河北清河），在安史之乱时就集聚了大量从江淮、河南地区征调来的布帛钱粮，被称为"天下北库"。可以说，隋唐时期的运河是整个封建王朝的经济大动脉，发挥着重要的漕运价值。

北宋是一个漕运业空前发展的时代，形成了以汴河为中心，包括黄河、汴河、蔡河、广济河在内的四通八达的漕运网。漕运量则从唐代每年100万石猛增至600万石，多的时候甚至能够达到800万石，创造了中国漕运史上的最高纪录。汴河在宋代不仅是开封赖以建都的生命线，也是东南物资漕运到东京的大动脉，不仅对京城汴梁有重要作用，而且还保证了北方边疆军事上的需要。

北宋灭亡后，出现了南北分裂的局面。汴河因为长期得不到疏浚，逐渐淤塞废弃。再加上北方地区长期战乱，人口稀少，经济衰落，导致了漕运逐渐走向低谷。

元朝定都大都（今北京市），大都成为全国的政治、经济中心，漕粮取之江南。最初采用水陆联运，由江淮溯黄河至封丘的中滦镇（今河南封丘县南），陆运180里至淇河镇（今河南浚县西南），再由御河（今卫河）至直沽（今天津市），再溯白河（今北运河）至通州，然后陆运至大都。其后为缩短运输路程和解决陆运的困难，自南向北先后开凿济州河、会通河、通惠河，形成了沟通南北的京杭大运河。但是由于新形成的京杭大运河改建为南北向，直通京都，再加上黄河频繁决溢，河南汴河漕运逐渐废弃。

在北宋初年所形成的"漕运四渠"（汴河、惠民河、广济河、金水河）中，惠民河的地位仅次于汴河，在我国水运史上也是一条较为重要的运河。整条运河以开封为中心分为上、下两个河段，上段河道称闵河，下段河道称蔡河。开凿惠民河有两个目的：一是解决蔡河的水源，二是

gathered during the Anshi Rebellion. It can be said that the canal in the Sui and Tang dynasties was the economic artery in the whole feudal dynasty and played a significant role in grain transport.

The Northern Song Dynasty witnessed an unprecedented development of canal transport industry as an extensive network of canal transport was formed, covering the Yellow River, the Bianhe River, the Caihe River and the Guangji River, with the Bianhe River as the center. The grain transport volume soared from 1 million dan per year to 6 million dan in the Tang Dynasty, and even reached 8 million dan in some cases, making it the highest record in the history of grain transport in China. The Bianhe River in the Song Dynasty was not only the lifeline for Kaifeng to be the capital, but also the main artery for supplies transported to Kaifeng from southeast China. It not only played an important role for the capital city, but also guaranteed the military needs in the northern frontier.

After the fall of the Northern Song Dynasty, the north and the south split up. The Bianhe River had not been dredged for a long time, so it gradually was silted up and abandoned. In addition, the long-term war in the north resulted in sparse population and economic decay, and the canal transport of grain eventually went to decline.

Established as the capital in the Yuan Dynasty, Dadu (now Beijing) became the political and economic center of the country. The grain that had been collected in taxes was shipped from the south of the Yangtze River to northern China. Initially, both water and land transport were adopted, starting from the Yangtze River and the Huaihe River to the town of Zhongluan of Fengqiu (now south of Fengqiu County, Henan Province), after 90 kilometers by land to Qihe Town (now southwest of Xunxian County, Henan Province), then to Zhigu (today's Tianjin City) by the Yuhe River (today's Weihe River), then to Tongzhou through the Baihe River (today's North Canal), and finally to Dadu by land. Later, in order to shorten the transportation distance and deal with the difficulties of land transport, the Jizhou River, the Huitong River and the Tonghui River were dug successively from the south to the north, thus the Beijing-Hangzhou Grand Canal was constructed to connect the north and the south of China. However, owing to the newly-constructed Beijing-Hangzhou Grand Canal running directly to the capital and the frequent overflow of the Yellow River, the canal transport by the

扩大漕运的地域范围。到了太平兴国六年（981年），惠民河所运送的漕粮已达到60万石。

惠民河在漕运价值上虽不如汴河，但在航运价值上却不低于汴河。汴河主要沟通东南地区的经济往来，惠民河却沟通了东南和西南两个地区。东南方向可以由蔡河经过颍河入淮河，随后分为两路进入长江。西南一路由开封向西南，经蔡河、沙河与南阳、湖北襄樊地区相通。惠民河自从开通后就一直是中原地区最重要的水运航道之一，尤其在北宋时期作用尤为突出，可以称为北宋王朝的生命线。但到了元代初年开始淤废，到了明代彻底丧失了漕运功能。

北宋开封及其运河水系
Kaifeng and its canal system of the Northern Song Dynasty

广济河是北宋"漕运四渠"之一，原本属于沁水支流。在五代时，为加强京师开封与山东北部滨海地区的物资运输，周世宗柴荣疏通汴水北入白沟，东流入济水，来沟通山东一带的漕运。河床也被展拓至五丈，所以俗称"五丈河"。北宋建隆二年（961年），宋太祖命人对这条河

Bianhe River in Henan province was gradually abandoned.

Among the four channels (the Bianhe River, the Huimin River, the Guangji River and the Jinshui River) built in the early Northern Song Dynasty, Huimin River ranked second only to Bianhe River, and it was also an important waterway in the history of water transport in China. The whole channel was divided into two sections with Kaifeng as the center. The upper section is called the Minhe River and the lower section the Caihe River. The Huimin River was dug for two purposes: one was to divert water to the Caihe River, the other was to expand the regional scope of grain transport. By the sixth year of Taiping Xingguo (981 AD), the grain transported by the Huimin River had reached 600 thousand dan.

The Huimin River was inferior to the Bianhe River in grain transport, but superior to it in shipping. The Bianhe River mainly worked for the economic exchanges in the southeast region, while the Huimin River connected the southeast and southwest. In the southeast, it passed from the Caihe River to the Huaihe River through the Yinghe River, and then separated into two parts to flow into the Yangtze River. In the southwest, it started from Kaifeng, ran through the Rivers of Caihe and Shahe and connected with Nanyang and Xiangfan in Hubei Province. Since its opening, the Huimin River was one of the most important watercourses in the Central Plains and was regarded as the lifeline of the country, especially in the Northern Song Dynasty. But it gradually silted up in the early Yuan Dynasty and completely lost the function of grain transport in the Ming Dynasty.

The Guangji River, one of the four rivers of grain transport in the Northern Song Dynasty, was originally a tributary of the Qinshui River. In the Five Dynasties Period (907-960 AD), in order to strengthen the transport of supplies between Kaifeng and the coastal area in the north of the Shandong Province, Chai Rong, Emperor Shizong of the Later Zhou Dynasty, ordered to dredge the Bianshui River to run to the north into Baigou and east into Jishui to connect with the grain transport in Shandong. The river, whose bed was also extended to five zhang, was commonly known as "the River of Five Zhang". In the second year of Jianlong of the Northern Song Dynasty (961 AD), Emperor Taizu ordered the river to be further built and other rivers to flow into it to increase the water volume. He also required that the river be dredged once a year. In the sixth year

道进一步修整,并让其他河流汇入河道,以增水量,并且要求每年要疏浚河道一次。开宝六年(973年),正式改名为广济河。广济河从开封出城后,通过大清河汇入渤海,将河南与山东通过水运联系起来,每年漕运可输送稻米62万石。宋人南迁之后,由于南北争战,汴渠水停顿,广济河也逐渐废弃。

在河南境内,濮阳市台前县境内的台前大运河是京杭大运河唯一流经今河南境的一段。大运河台前段全长10多公里,南从山东省东平县十里铺村进入,向北进入山东。台前大运河自元朝通航以来,历经元明清三代,数百年间一直是漕运的干道。当时,这里舟楫往来,集市星布,商贩云集。苏州的丝绸、杭州的茶叶以及江南水乡洁白如玉的大米等,源源不断地从这里穿越黄河,送往北京、天津。而京津的洋货、宝器以及后来的海盐等货物又从这里南下江浙。同时,历史上曾有无数来自日本、朝鲜、印度和阿拉伯、欧洲等地的使者、高僧、商人,通过运河亲身了解着当时的中国;而一批又一批的瓷器、丝绸等中国商品和书籍也经由运河出海,运往世界各地。历史发展证明:大运河自开通以后,不仅把我国的南方和北方连接为一体,而且也成了中外经济文化交流的重要纽带。

of Kaibao (973 AD), the river was formally renamed the Guangji River. After running out of Kaifeng, the Guangji River entered the Bohai Sea through the Daqing River, which linked Henan and Shandong by the waterways. Every year 620 thousand dan of rice was transported through the Guangji River. After the people of the Song Dynasty moved to the south, the Bianqu Channel stopped flowing due to the wars between the north and the south, and the Guangji River was gradually abandoned.

The Taiqian Canal in Taiqian County of Puyang City in Henan Province is the only part of the Beijing-Hangzhou Grand Canal that flows through Henan Province. It is over 10 kilometers long, flowing northward into Shandong Province from Shilipu Village, Dongping County, Shandong Province. Since its navigation in the Yuan Dynasty, the Taiqian Canal was the main canal for grain transport for hundreds of years through the Yuan, Ming and Qing dynasties. At that time, there were numerous markets along both sides of the Canal. Silk from Suzhou, tea from Hangzhou and rice from the south of the Yangtze River were transported from here to Beijing and Tianjin through the Yellow River in a steady flow. Foreign goods, treasures and sea salt from Beijing and Tianjin were transported to Jiangsu and Zhejiang. At the same time, numerous emissaries, eminent monks and businessmen from Japan, Korea, India, Arabia, Europe and other places came to learn about China. Batches of books, porcelain and silk were also shipped to other parts of the world through the Canal. Historical development has proved that since its opening, the Grand Canal not only connected the south and the north of China as a whole, but also became an important link of economic and cultural exchanges between China and foreign countries.

二、运河的历史价值

中国大运河是世界上开凿时间最早、规模最大、线路最长、延续时间最久的人工运河，是举世闻名的伟大工程和文化遗产，凝聚着中华民族的智慧与创造力。以洛阳为中心和枢纽的隋唐大运河不仅首次连接钱塘江、长江、淮河、黄河、海河五大水系，而且成为中国古代特别是隋、唐、宋时期中国南北交通的大动脉，在国家统一、农业灌溉、文化交流、区域融合等方面发挥了重要作用。

从历史上看，大运河对国家的稳定和政治局势稳固十分重要。尤其是隋唐大运河的开凿与利用，都是围绕着巩固和强化皇朝统治而展开的，其最直接的目的就是出于军事需要和经济需求。隋代统一中国后，隋炀帝为了确保江南漕粮及时北调以满足皇室朝廷及大批军队的日常所需，使中央政令通达南北，下令修建运河。唐朝是真正发挥运河漕运作用的王朝，大运河将富庶的江南地区与国家政治中心相连，使得唐王朝的经济文化都呈现出昌盛发达的景象。元朝开凿济州河、通惠河等运道，从大运河北调的南粮达到全国总税粮的六分之五。明朝因为实行海禁，大运河成为唯一的南北水运通道，成为国家的"生命线"。在一定程度上可以说，谁控制了运河，谁就能建立起稳定的对全国的政治统治。因此，大运河就成了维系中央集权和中国大一统局面的政治纽带，使隋唐以后政治中心逐渐北移的历代皇朝呈现出强烈的大一统特征，特别是元朝实现全国统一以后，直至明清两朝，中国再也没有出现大的分裂，从而奠定了祖国大一统局面的坚实基础。大运河的贯通，大一统局面的形成，加强了民族间的紧密联系与融合，进一步增强了民族团结和中华民族的凝聚力和向心力。

大运河的开通与农田水利建设事业紧密相关。在开拓航道的同时，以减少水患和农田灌溉为主要内容的农田水利工程兴建起来，使运河

II. The Historical Significance of the Canal

The Grand Canal is the oldest man-made canal in the world with the largest scale, longest route and longest duration. It is a world-renowned great project and cultural heritage that embodies the wisdom and creativity of the Chinese nation. The Sui-Tang Grand Canal, with Luoyang as the center and hub, not only connected the Qiantang River, the Yangtze River, the Huaihe River, the Yellow River and the Haihe River for the first time, but also became the major artery between the north and the south in ancient China, especially in the Sui, Tang and Song dynasties. It played a significant role in national unification, agricultural irrigation, cultural exchanges and regional integration.

Historically, the Grand Canal has been of great importance to national stability. In particular, the building and utilization of the Grand Canal in the Sui and Tang dynasties both centered on consolidating and strengthening the rule of the imperial dynasty, and its most direct purpose was to meet the military and economic needs. After the unification of China in the Sui Dynasty, Emperor Yang of the Sui Dynasty ordered the construction of the canal to ensure the timely transfer of grain from the south of the Yangtze River to northern China to meet the daily needs of the imperial government and a large number of troops. The Tang Dynasty was the dynasty in which the canal transport was truly brought into full play. The Grand Canal connected the rich regions in the south of the Yangtze River with the political center of the country, contributing to the economic and cultural prosperity in the Tang Dynasty. The Jizhou Channel, the Tonghui Channel and other channels were built in the Yuan Dynasty, through which five-sixths of the national total tax grain was transferred to the north from the south. The Grand Canal, the lifeline of the whole nation, became the only waterway between the north and the south in the Ming Dynasty because of the prohibition of sea transportation. To a certain extent, he who controlled the Canal could establish stable political rule over the whole country. The Grand Canal, therefore, was a political link to maintain centralization and unification for the whole country. After the Sui and Tang dynasties, the political center gradually moved northward, and the imperial governments showed strong characteristics of unification. Especially after the national unification of the Yuan Dynasty up

区域的水利田获得大幅度的扩展,尤其是江南的圩田、北方的淤田、各类的水利田以及沿运地区的官府屯田和营田等,都有显著的增加。隋唐以后,运河的贯通直接推动了南北方农业生产技术的广泛交流、南北方农作物品种的相互移植与栽培,促进了南北方经济作物的普遍种植,加速了南北方商品农业经济的发展,使运河地区的生产力水平获得显著提高,也使运河区域成为全国人口最稠密的地区,从而确保农业经济的稳步发展。

大运河具有文化融通的作用。众所周知,我国疆域辽阔,东西南北经济社会发展不均衡,从而出现具有浓厚地域特色的文化。大运河文化是以黄河流域文化为核心,以长安、洛阳、开封、杭州、北京为中心,与海河、淮河、长江、钱塘江共同融合出的独特的江河文化,并紧密与中原文化相承。作为漕运主干道,大运河北接国家首都,南连江南地区,有力推动了中华民族政治、经济、文化大一统的发展,促进形成了多元一体的华夏文明。齐鲁文化、燕赵文化、楚汉文化、淮扬文化、吴越文化等多重区域文化在大运河的融合发展,成为全民族共同的精神财富。

大运河文化以其博大的包容性和统一性、广阔的扩散性和开放性、强大的凝聚力和向心力,不仅加强了中国传统思想文化发源地齐鲁地区与中原地区、江南地区的文化交融,而且把汉唐的长安、洛阳,两宋的开封、杭州和金、元、明、清的北京为首的文化中心连为一体,区域文化的差异不断减少而呈现出共同的文化特征,从而使文化融合为中华民族的多元一体的大一统文化;同时也使运河区域成为人才荟萃之地、文风昌盛之区。大运河的水哺育了许多著名的政治家、军事家、思想家、科学家、发明家、文学家和艺术家。如以夏商周文化、汉魏文化、唐宋文化为代表的中原传统文化,以老子、庄子、张衡、许慎、张仲景、吴道子、杜甫、韩愈、岳飞、朱载堉为代表的中原名人,以及以武术文化、根亲文化、农耕文化、黄河文化、老子文化等为代表的中原社会文化。它们不但对运河文化的发展做出了重大的贡献,而且对中国历史乃至世

to the Ming and Qing dynasties, China was no longer split up, which laid a solid foundation for the unification of the country. The connection of the Grand Canal and the formation of the national unification strengthened the close ties and integration among all the nationalities, and further strengthened the national unification and the cohesion and centripetal force of the Chinese nation.

The opening of the Grand Canal is closely related to the construction of irrigation and water conservancy. At the same time as the Canal was built, water conservancy projects with the main purpose of controlling floods and irrigating farmland were built along the Grand Canal, which greatly expanded the water conservancy field in the Canal zone, especially the dike paddy field in the south of the Yangtze River and sediment field in the north. The government wasteland and battalion cropland in the area along the Canal were also increased significantly. After the Sui and Tang dynasties, the connection of the Canal directly promoted the extensive exchange of agricultural production technology and the mutual transplantation and cultivation of crop varieties between the north and the south, increased the general planting of economic crops and accelerated the development of commercial agricultural economy in the north and south. It improved the productivity of the Canal region significantly, making it the most densely populated region in the country and ensuring the steady development of the agricultural economy.

The Grand Canal played a vital role in cultural interactions. As is known to all, China is a country with a vast territory and uneven economic and social development across the country, leading to the emergence of cultures with strong regional characteristics. The Grand Canal culture is a unique river culture, with the Yellow River Basin culture as its core and Chang'an, Luoyang, Kaifeng, Hangzhou and Beijing as its geographical roots. It is integrated with the culture of Haihe River, Huaihe River, Yangtze River and Qiantang River, and closely inherited from Central Plains culture. As the main channel of grain transport, the Grand Canal connected the national capital in the north with the regions in the south of the Yangtze River, which effectively promoted the political, economic and cultural unity of the Chinese nation and the formation of a pluralistic and integrated Chinese civilization. The integrated development of Qilu culture, Yanzhao culture, Chuhan culture, Huaiyang culture, Wuyue culture and other regional cultures along the Grand Canal has become the common spiritual wealth of the whole nation.

开凿大运河
The construction of the Grand Canal

界历史都有着广泛而深远的影响。

　　一部大运河变迁史，揭示一个亘古不变的事实：历代运河的开凿、整修都需要国家投入大量的财力和人力，所以大规模地开凿、整修运河，常常在政治比较清明、国家富强时期。反过来说，运河的开凿和整修对国家的繁荣富强、统治的巩固和稳定，又起着积极作用。而当政治腐败、国家贫弱时，不仅没有或很少有开凿运河的盛举，即使前代开凿的运河，也往往难以保全。一旦运河不能通航，必将给国家带来不可估量的损失或危害，甚至导致皇朝的灭亡。所以中国古代的运河问题，不仅是一个水运航道的问题，涉及国计民生的经济问题，而且还是一个政治问题，对历代统治者来说，也是一个政治生命线的问题。

The Grand Canal culture, with its broad inclusiveness and unity, broad diffusion and openness, strong cohesion and centripetal force, not only strengthened the cultural integration between the Qilu region, the cradle of Chinese traditional thought, and the Central Plains and the regions in the south of the Yangtze River, but also combined the cultural centers headed by Chang'an and Luoyang of the Han and Tang dynasties, Kaifeng and Hangzhou of the Song Dynasty and Beijing of the Jin, Yuan, Ming and Qing dynasties, thus steadily decreasing differences in regional cultures and presenting the common cultural characteristics, so that the culture integrated into the Chinese nation as a pluralistic integration of a great unified one. At the same time, the Canal area became a place for various talents. The Grand Canal has nurtured many famous statesmen, militarists, thinkers, scientists, inventors, writers and artists. Examples are the Central Plains traditional culture represented by the Xia, Shang and Zhou culture, Han and Wei culture, Tang and Song culture, the celebrities in the Central Plains represented by Lao Tzu, Zhuang Tzu, Zhang Heng, Xu Shen, Zhang Zhongjing, Wu Daozi, Du Fu, Han Yu, Yue Fei and Zhu Zaiyu, and the social culture of the Central Plains represented by Wushu culture, root culture, farming culture, Yellow River culture, Lao Tzu culture, etc. The talents of the Grand Canal area not only made great contributions to the development of Canal culture, but also had extensive and far-reaching influence on Chinese history and even world history.

The history of the Grand Canal reveals the invariable fact that the construction and renovation of the canals in successive dynasties required the state to invest a large amount of financial and human resources, so the large-scale construction and renovation of the canals were often carried out during the period when the state was relatively prosperous and peaceful. On the other hand, the construction and renovation of the canals played a positive role for the prosperity of the country as well as the consolidation and stability of its rule. When the government was corrupt and weak, not only no or little canal construction was undertaken, but even the canals of previous generations were often difficult to preserve. Once the canal was not navigable, it would certainly bring inestimable loss or harm to the country, and even lead to the demise of the imperial dynasty. Therefore, the Canal in ancient China was not only related to the national waterway, but also connected with the national economy and people's livelihood. It also affected politics and was a political lifeline for the rulers of successive dynasties.

三、运河的精神价值

如果说长城是凝固的历史,那么大运河就是流动的文化,是活着的世界级人类文化遗产。中国大运河的开凿、发展和兴盛的过程就是一部中华民族的文明史,同时也是中华民族的文化形成、发展和完善的历史,体现了不同历史时期的文化精神融合,是实现国家认同的重要文化纽带。如果说长江和黄河是中华民族自强不息精神的代表,那么大运河就是中华民族厚德载物精神的诠释。

大运河精神是中华优秀传统文化的重要组成部分。从世界运河范围看,大运河是人工河流,比自然的产物更能承载历史的赠予、国家的意志,是制度与文化的产物,是实现国家认同的有力媒介。中国大运河是中华文明的重要标识,是中国文化的记忆之场,承载着中国人的文化乡愁,积淀着中华民族几千年来最深沉的精神追求,是中华民族的守望者,蕴含着中华文化振兴的密码。大运河开凿于春秋,完成于隋,繁荣于唐宋,取直于元,疏通于明清,是生生不息、从未断绝的中华文明生命力的镜像。大运河是中华文化多元一体化的象征,它内蕴的"以人为本"的核心思想、"家国情怀"的责任担当、"海纳百川"的文化取向、"和而不同"的民族性格,立体化地呈现了建设美好家园、谋求和平发展的国家形象。

自强不息精神是大运河精神的源。大运河文化中蕴含的交流包容、协作共享、自强不息、吃苦耐劳的精神基因已深深融入中华民族精神血液中。秦汉时期江南运河的开凿、隋代南北大运河的形成、明清京杭大运河的蓬勃等,促使中国大运河成为世界上空间跨度最大、使用时间最久的运河。运河是流经区域自然地理状况异常复杂的人工运河,这也充分体现了中华民族不畏艰难、顽强拼搏、生生不息的奋斗进取精神。

守正创新精神是大运河精神的根。两千多年来,伴随着大运河的水环境变迁,大运河的开凿技术、管理制度、治水思想也与时俱进。如为

III. The Spiritual Significance of the Canal

If the Great Wall represents a frozen history, the Grand Canal shows a flowing culture and a living world-class human cultural heritage. The building, development and prosperity of the Grand Canal in China is not only a history of Chinese civilization, but also a history of formation, development and improvement of Chinese culture. Reflecting the cultural and spiritual integration of different historical periods, the Grand Canal is an important cultural link to achieve national identity. If the Yangtze River and the Yellow River represent the Chinese nation's spirit of unremitting self-improvement, the Grand Canal is the interpretation of the Chinese nation's spirit of social commitment.

The Grand Canal spirit is an important part of the excellent traditional culture of the Chinese nation. Broadly speaking, the canal is an artificial river, which can bear national will more than the natural rivers. As the product of Chinese culture, it is a powerful medium to realize the national identity. The Grand Canal is an important symbol of Chinese civilization and a place that carries the memories of Chinese culture and nostalgia of Chinese people, embodying the deepest spiritual pursuit of the Chinese nation for thousands of years. The canal, the watchman of the Chinese nation, contains the code for the rejuvenation of Chinese culture. The Grand Canal was started in the Spring and Autumn Period, completed in the Sui Dynasty, flourished in the Tang and Song dynasties, straightened out in the Yuan Dynasty, and dredged in the Ming and Qing dynasties. It is the symbol of the multi-cultural integration of Chinese culture, containing the core idea of "people oriented", the responsibility of "family and country", the cultural orientation of "tolerance to diversities" and the national character of "harmony in diversity". It presents a three-dimensional national image of building a beautiful homeland and fostering peaceful development.

The spirit of unremitting self-improvement is the source of the spirit of the Grand Canal. The spirit gene of communication and inclusiveness, cooperation and sharing, unremitting self-improvement, and hard work embodied in the Grand Canal culture has been deeply incorporated into the spirit of the Chinese nation. The building of the Jiangnan Canal during the Qin and Han dynasties, the

了解决黄河泥沙，宋代劳动人民在实践中创造了堰坝设施，实现引潮、蓄水、节水和输水等的多重功能，成为当时领先世界的标志性工程。与此同时，运河的开凿整修技术也日渐成熟，运河的管理日臻完善。元明清时期，不仅在解决运河水源，保护河堤，开凿河道，利用各种闸、堰以控制调节运河水量等关键技术上有重大创新突破，涌现出郭守敬、潘季驯、靳辅等一批卓有成就的水运专家，而且还完善了各个职责分明的运河管理机构，制定了较为严密的规章制度，以确保运河的航运畅通，极大地发挥着运河在漕运等方面的功能。

郭守敬
Guo Shoujing

兼容并蓄精神是大运河精神的魂。中国大运河从古到今绵延千百年，促进了不同地域间文化的交流、沟通和融合，推动了中华民族多元一体

formation of the Grand Canal in the Sui Dynasty, the prosperity of the Beijing-Hangzhou Grand Canal in the Ming and Qing dynasties, make the Grand Canal the longest and oldest canal in the world. The Canal flows through extremely complicated regions geographically, which fully embodies the Chinese nation's enterprising spirit of fearless of difficulties, tenacious struggle and continuous production.

The spirit of integrity and innovation is the root of the spirit of the Grand Canal. Over the past two thousand years, along with the changes of the water environment of the Grand Canal, the Canal's digging technology, management system and water control thought have also kept pace with the times. For example, in order to solve the sediment of the Yellow River, the laboring people in the Song Dynasty created barrage facilities in practice, which carried out the functions of attracting tide, storing water, saving water and carrying water, etc., and became a landmark project leading the world at that time. At the same time, the Canal building and renovation technology also became increasingly mature, and the Canal management is becoming increasingly perfect. In the Yuan, Ming and Qing dynasties, there were significant innovation breakthroughs in key technologies, such as solving the water source of the Canal, protecting the river bank, digging the river course, using all kinds of locks and weirs to control and regulate the water volume of the Canal, thus creating a group of accomplished experts in water transport like Guo Shoujing, Pan Jixun and Jin Fu. At the same time, the Canal management organizations with distinct responsibilities were improved, and strict rules and regulations were formulated to ensure the smooth transporting of the Canal, which played a significant role in grain transportation.

The spirit of inclusiveness is the soul of the Grand Canal. The Grand Canal, running for more than two thousand years, has promoted the cultural exchanges, communication and integration between different regions, and facilitated the emergence of the diversified and integrated cultural form of the Chinese nation. It flows through most parts of China, and the Wuyue culture, the Huaiyang culture, the Central Plains culture, the Qilu culture, the Yanzhao culture, the Beijing and Tianjin culture all add splendor to each other, forming a poetic living environment, unique architectural style, exquisite craftsmanship, numerous celebrity stories, rich folk art and folk customs. The Grand Canal integrates

文化格局出现。大运河流经中国大部分地区，吴越文化、淮扬文化、中原文化、齐鲁文化、燕赵文化、京津文化等交相辉映，形成了诗意的人居环境、独特的建筑风格、精湛的手工技艺、众多的名人故事以及丰富的民间艺术和民风民俗。流动的大运河融合交汇制度文化、精神文化和社会文化，从而形成了独具标识的大运河文化。大运河文化既具有中国文化的一般特性，又包含明显的地域特色，是多元一体的文化。与此同时，中国大运河与陆上丝绸之路、海上丝绸之路相通，把中国内地与海外世界各地联系起来。盛唐时期，大批遣唐使经大运河来到长安。当时的长安因大运河成了中外经济文化的中心。

　　大运河沿线物质文化遗产超过1200项，国家级非物质文化遗产450余项，大运河是一条中华民族精神的大河，流淌着中华民族的历史基因,承载着中华民族的悠久历史和文明。1000多年前,大运河贯通南北，成为世界上最长的人工河。如今，大运河的繁华早已成为历史，但她留下的丰富遗产，却沉淀为流动的文化，饱含中国优秀传统文化的基因，在历史长河中闪烁时代价值。

institutional culture with spiritual culture and social culture, thus forming the distinctive Grand Canal culture. The Grand Canal culture not only has the general characteristics of Chinese culture, but also contains the obvious regional characteristics. It is a diverse and integrated culture. At the same time, the Grand Canal was connected with the Overland Silk Road and the Maritime Silk Road, connecting China's mainland with the rest of the world. In the flourishing period of the Tang Dynasty, a large number of envoys came to Chang'an via the Grand Canal. At that time, Chang'an became the economic and cultural center of the world because of the Grand Canal.

Along the Grand Canal, there are more than 1,200 items of tangible cultural heritage, and more than 450 items of national intangible cultural heritage. The Grand Canal is a great waterway of Chinese national spirit, flowing with the historical genes of the Chinese nation and carrying the long history and civilization of the Chinese nation. More than 1,000 years ago, the Grand Canal, running from the north to the south, was the longest man-made river in the world. Nowadays, the prosperity of the Grand Canal has long been a thing of the past, but its heritage has become a flowing culture, full of the genes of excellent traditional Chinese culture, which has been flashing with the value of the times in the long history.

四、运河的时代价值

大运河持续运行两千余年,是我国古代最伟大的水利工程之一,与长城共同搭建起中国精神的"人"字结构。大运河在人类社会发展史上留下了不可磨灭的印记,充分显示了中华民族的智慧与勇气。大运河是不可替代的文化资源,是中华水文化传承的载体,是流动的文化,是中国传统制度文化、技术文化、社会文化的集合体,是国家的标志性遗产,是中华民族活着、流动的精神家园。

大运河连通着海河、黄河、淮河、长江、钱塘江五大水系,其与长江的纵横轴向式结合,在空间上与"一带一路"可以形成水陆两路兼济的双重对接,是推进"一带一路"建设的重要切入点。进入实现中华民族伟大复兴中国梦的新时代,续写大运河宏伟历史诗篇,以高度的文化自信传承与弘扬大运河文化,具有极大的时代价值和现实意义。

2014年6月22日,中国大运河在第38届世界遗产大会上获准列入世界遗产名录。大运河遗产分布在中国2个直辖市、6个省、25个地级市,包括闸、堤、坝、桥、水城门、纤道、码头、险工等运河水工遗存,以及仓窖、衙署、驿站、行宫、会馆、钞关等大运河的配套设施和管理设施,和一部分与大运河文化意义密切相关的古建筑、历史文化街区等。河南是隋唐大运河的源头和核心区域,是大运河河道路线最长、流经古都最多、运河遗产最为丰富的省份,是华夏历史文明的重要组成部分。可以说,人类文明史就是运河的发展史。

作为中国大运河重要组成部分的大运河河南段既是五大片区之———隋唐大运河河南片区,又是六大高地之———中原文化高地,涉及郑州、洛阳、安阳、鹤壁、商丘和滑县等6市县,涵盖了河道、码头、河堤等完整的遗产类型,见证了大运河从开凿、发展到繁荣、没落的历

IV. The Epochal Significance of the Canal

The Grand Canal, which has been in operation for more than 2,000 years, is one of the greatest water projects in ancient China. Like the Great Wall, it helped to foster a spirit of cooperation and hard-work of the Chinese people. The Grand Canal is an indelible part in the history of human development, which fully demonstrated the wisdom and courage of the Chinese nation. As an irreplaceable cultural resource, the Grand Canal is the carrier of Chinese water culture inheritance. It is not only a combination of traditional Chinese institutional culture, technological culture and social culture, but also the iconic national heritage and the spiritual homeland of the Chinese nation.

The Grand Canal connects the Haihe River, the Yellow River, the Huaihe River, the Yangtze River and the Qiantang River. The combination of the Grand Canal and the Yangtze River in the vertical and horizontal axis can form a double linking with "the Belt and Road Initiative" in space, which is an important entry point to promote the construction of "the Initiative". After entering a new era to realize the Chinese dream of the great rejuvenation of the Chinese nation, it is of great era value and practical significance to continue to write magnificent historical poems on the Grand Canal and carry forward the Grand Canal culture with high cultural self-confidence.

On June 22, 2014, the Grand Canal was included in the World Heritage List at the 38th World Heritage Conference. The Grand Canal heritage is distributed in 25 prefecture-level cities in 6 provinces and 2 municipalities directly under the central government of China, including the Canal hydraulic work remains, such as sluice, dike, dam, bridge, water gate, towpath, wharf and dangerous sections as well as the supporting facilities and management facilities of the Grand Canal, such as the warehouse cellar, local magistrate's office, temporary imperial palace, guildhall, tax bureau, etc., and a part of the ancient buildings and historical and cultural blocks that are closely related to the cultural significance of the Grand Canal. Henan, the source and core area of the Grand Canal in Sui and Tang dynasties and an important part of Chinese historical civilization, is the province with the longest Canal route, the most ancient capitals and the richest Canal heritage. It can be said

大运河河南段示意图
Sketch map of Henan section of the Grand Canal

史进程,具有重要的历史和文化价值。

《大运河文化保护传承利用规划纲要》指出,要强化大运河精神内涵的挖掘,结合时代条件加以继承和发扬,赋予其新的时代含义和文化价值,让中华文化展现出永久魅力和时代风采。为永续大运河文脉,河南省也是响应国家号召,提出保护传承利用大运河文化、建设大运河绿色生态廊道的要求,使"千年运河"文化旅游品牌享誉中外。投资15亿元的隋唐大运河国家文化公园项目在洛阳市老城区集中开工,是讲好河南大运河故事、面向世界打造开放型文化高地的重要举措。

总的来说,河南大运河作为大运河的根脉和原点,见证了中国文化的鼎盛繁荣。河南将更加突出隋唐大运河的盛世文化符号,在全国大运河文化保护传承利用工作中发挥积极作用,为实现中华民族伟大复兴的中国梦贡献更多的力量。

that the history of human civilization is the history of the canal.

The Henan section of the Grand Canal, an important part of the Grand Canal, is not only one of the five districts, the Henan district of the Sui-Tang Grand Canal , but also one of six highlands—highland of Central Plains culture, involving Zhengzhou, Luoyang, Anyang, Hebi, Shangqiu and Huaxian County, covering the whole heritage types such as river courses, wharves and embankments, witnessing the historical process of the Grand Canal from digging and development to prosperity and decline, which is of great historical and cultural significance.

It is pointed out in *The Outline of the Plan for the Protection, Inheritance and Utilization of the Grand Canal Culture* that it is necessary to strengthen the exploration of the spiritual connotations of the Grand Canal, inherit and develop it in the light of the times, and endow it with new era connotations and cultural significance, so that Chinese culture will show its permanent charm. In order to maintain the culture of the Grand Canal, Henan Province also responded to the national call and proposed to protect, inherit and utilize the Grand Canal culture and build the green ecological corridor of the Grand Canal, so as to make the cultural tourism brand of Millennium Canal well known at home and abroad. The Sui-Tang Grand Canal National Cultural Park project with an investment of 1.5 billion *yuan* was launched in the old city of Luoyang, which is an important measure to tell the story of Henan section of the Grand Canal to build an open cultural highland for the world.

In short, as the origin of the Grand Canal, the Henan section has witnessed the great prosperity of Chinese culture. In the future, Henan people will make greater effort to highlight the cultural symbols of the Sui-Tang Grand Canal and play a role in the preservation and utilization of the Grand Canal throughout the country.

第三章

运河文化形态

Chapter 3

The Cultural Forms of the Canal

运河的繁华与兴衰，给中国留下了独特的大运河文化。大运河沿线孕育了吴越、淮扬、中原、齐鲁、燕赵、京津等六大文化形态。河南大运河文化是中原文化的重要组成部分。河南大运河沿岸的洛阳、开封、郑州是运河历史古都文化名城，浚县古城、滑县道口古镇、开封朱仙镇、南乐元村是运河流经的古城镇和古村落，洛阳隋唐大运河博物馆、巩义洛口仓和商丘火神台庙会是延续千年文脉的重要符号，也是讲好运河故事，让中原更加出彩的文化资源。

一、运河古都

运河的开通与兴盛，带动了都城繁荣和辉煌。如乳汁一般的运河水，不仅承载着南来北往的各种船只，而且孕育和滋润了沿岸的一座座城市，使它们犹如镶嵌在彩带上的一颗颗明珠，争奇斗艳，璀璨夺目。在中国古都学会命名的八大古都历史文化名城中，河南占四个城市，分别是洛阳、开封、安阳和郑州。河南古都城市也是隋唐大运河通济渠、永济渠及京杭大运河中的会通河在河南境内流经的核心地区。大运河主河道流经的洛阳、开封、郑州也成为运河都城，留下了深刻运河文化烙印，是河南走向世界的城市名片。

当年隋炀帝定都洛阳，在营建洛阳的同时就着手修建大运河，形成了以洛阳为中心的水运网，南通今杭州，北达今北京，西经黄河到长安。作为隋唐大运河和北宋运河的重要枢纽，汴河对后世也产生了深远的影响。汴河既是开封赖以建都的生命线，也是东南地区物资漕运东京的大动脉。它不仅为京城的物资供应提供了有效保障，而且为北方边疆军事需要提供了重要保障。

1. 洛阳

洛阳古称雒阳、神都，是隋唐大运河的中心枢纽城市，位于河南省

The prosperity and decline of the Grand Canal have left China with unique culture. Along the Grand Canal, six cultural forms like Wuyue, Huaiyang, Central Plains, Qilu, Yanzhao, Jingjin cultures were born. Henan Grand Canal culture is an important part of Central Plains culture. Luoyang, Kaifeng and Zhengzhou along the Grand Canal are the famous historical ancient capitals and cultural cities. The ancient city of Xunxian County, the ancient Town of Daokou of Huaxian County, Zhuxianzhen of Kaifeng and Yuancun Town of Nanle County are the ancient towns and villages that the Canal ran through. The Sui-Tang Grand Canal Museum in Luoyang, the Luokou Granary in Gongyi and the Huoshentai Temple Fair in Shangqiu are important symbols of the cultural context lasting for thousands of years. They are also the cultural resources to tell the story of the Canal well and make the Central Plains more outstanding.

Ⅰ. The Ancient Capitals along the Canal

The opening and prosperity of the Canal led to the prosperity and glory of ancient capitals. It not only carried various ships from the south to the north and vice versa, but also nurtured cities which were like pearls inlaid on the ribbon, colorful, brilliant and dazzling. Among the eight famous historical and cultural cities named by the Chinese Society of Ancient Capitals, there are four cities from Henan, namely Luoyang, Kaifeng, Anyang and Zhengzhou. The ancient capital cities of Henan Province are also located in the core area where the Tongji Channel and Yongji Channel of the Sui-Tang Grand Canal and the Huitong River of Beijing-Hangzhou Grand Canal meet in Henan Province. Luoyang, Zhengzhou and Kaifeng, through which the main watercourse of the Grand Canal flows, have also become the Canal capitals, retaining a profound Canal culture and becoming the leading cities of Henan.

While Emperor Yang of the Sui Dynasty made Luoyang the capital, he ordered to build the Grand Canal so as to form a water transportation network with Luoyang as the center, which reached Hangzhou to the south, Beijing to the north, and Chang'an to the west by the Yellow River. As an important hub of the Grand Canal in the Sui and Tang dynasties and the Northern Song Dynasty, the Bianhe River also had a profound influence on later generations. The Bianhe

西部的伊洛盆地，南临伊阙，北倚邙山，东西分据虎牢、函谷两关，自古便有"八关都邑，八面环山，五水绕洛城"的说法。

仁寿四年（604年）七月，隋炀帝正式即位。605年3月17日，隋炀帝下令大规模营建东京洛阳，在汉魏旧城西重筑新城，并将全国数万家富商大贾迁到洛阳。隋炀帝在营建东京的同时，又从洛阳的西苑引涧水和洛水到黄河。稍后大运河和永济渠的修建，使洛阳成为全国水陆交通的中心，成为著名的商业都市。洛阳城内有居民区120坊和丰都、大同、通远等三个"市"。三市占地广阔，商业繁荣，最大的丰都市方圆八里，据说市内有120个行业，3000余家店铺，周围还有400余家商店。

"居中而治，四塞险固，山河拱戴"是中国封建王朝建都选址的基本准则。纵观历代都城，几乎无一例外地依山傍水而建，说明古代都城的选址对于以山川河流为载体的水源的高度依赖。隋唐洛阳城的水系由自然水系与人工水系两大部分组成。

自然水系有洛水、谷水、伊水、瀍水。洛水从洛阳城西南部流入，

隋唐洛阳城
Luoyang City in Sui and Tang dynasties

River was not only the lifeline of Kaifeng, but also the main artery of supplies transported to it from the southeast regions. It provided effective guarantee for the supplies of the capital, and for the military needs in the northern border as well.

1. Luoyang

Luoyang was the central hub city of the Sui-Tang Grand Canal, located in the Yiluo Basin in the west of Henan Province. It faces Yique to the south, leans against the Mangshan Mountain in the north, and occupies the Hulaoguan Pass and Hanguguan Pass in the east and west respectively. Since ancient times there has been a saying "The capital city has eight passes, surrounded by mountains and rivers on four sides".

In July 604, Emperor Yang of the Sui Dynasty ascended the throne. On March 17, 605, he ordered to build Luoyang. A new city in the west of the old one was built and tens of thousands of wealthy merchants from all over the country were moved to Luoyang. While Dongjing was under construction, Emperor Yang ordered to divert the Jianshui River and Luoshui River from Xiyuan in Luoyang to the Yellow River. Later, with the construction of the Grand Canal and the Yongji Channel, Luoyang became the center of land and water transportation and a famous commercial city in China. Inside the city, there were 120 residential blocks and 3 markets, namely Fengdu, Datong and Tongyuan. The three markets covered a vast area with flourishing commerce. The largest one, Fengdu Market, extended for 4 kilometers in every direction. There were 120 businesses and more than 3,000 shops in it and over 400 stores around it.

"To rule in the center, with solid bulwarks around, surrounded by mountains and rivers" is the basic criteria for the site selection of the capitals of feudal dynasties in China. Throughout history, capitals were built almost without exception by mountains and rivers, indicating that the site selection of ancient capitals was highly dependent on the water source carried by mountains and rivers. The water system of Luoyang City in Sui and Tang dynasties was composed of natural water system and artificial water system.

The natural water system included the Luoshui River, the Gushui River, the Yishui River and the Chanshui River. The Luoshui River flowed from the

东流到皇城南门端门外,再自西向东将整个城分为南、北两个区域。城内的供水以洛水为主要水源,洛水自西向东横贯全城。谷水自洛阳城西北向东南流经神都苑,在上阳宫北部分成了三支,第一支向东引入宫城,第二、三支分别在上阳宫东西侧汇入洛水。谷水是当时皇家园林的重要水源,最终汇入洛水。伊水自城之南分为两支北流入外郭城,于城内合为一股,经城内数坊又过永通门、建春门向东流入南运渠,为洛阳城东南生活用水与漕运的重要组成部分。瀍水在洛水之北,由东城之东第三南北街最北的修义坊西南流入城中,向南流至东城之东第二南北街最南的归义坊流入漕渠。

人工水系主要有漕渠、泄城渠、写口渠。漕渠与洛水、瀍水、泄城渠相连,最终汇入洛水。漕渠是隋唐洛阳城连接大运河的命脉,也是交通要道。泄城渠由城北入城,可以连通含嘉仓城与漕渠。写口渠是连接泄城渠与漕渠的一段人工渠。

作为东都的洛阳选择利用多条自然水系和人工水系组成网状水系,采用了以洛水为主干的水系规划,其他水系汇入洛水而归于黄河,形成了极具特色的城市水利。洛水穿城开辟了我国古代都城建设的新纪元,为后世的开封城、北京城水系穿城奠定了基础。

隋唐大运河的开通使洛阳的交通变得非常便利,再加上丝绸之路也通过洛阳,一条贯穿南北、一条连通东西的交通要道在洛阳交汇,由此形成洛阳城内繁华的商业大都市,带动了洛阳城经济和商业的繁荣,洛阳成为当时国内最大的商业大都市,同时也成为世界上著名的商业大都市。商业的繁荣也带动了南北文化的交流与融合,造就了独特的河洛文化。

唐中叶安史之乱以后,洛阳遭到严重破坏,保存下来的建筑物不到原来的1/10,洛阳开始趋于衰落。五代时虽有后梁、后唐、后晋(以洛阳为都约不到两年)建都于此,仍十分衰蔽。北宋时,洛阳一度有所恢复,成为北宋学术文化中心。但北宋灭亡以后,洛阳日渐衰落。

southwest of Luoyang City to the east of the gate outside the southern end of the imperial city, and then divided the whole city into the north and the south by running from the west to the east. The main source of the city's water supply was the Luoshui River, running from the west to the east across the city. The Gushui River flowed from the northwest of Luoyang City to the southeast through Shenduyuan and divided into three branches in the north of Shangyang Palace. The first branch flowed eastward to the Palace, and the second and third branches merged into the Luoshui River on the east and west sides of Shangyang Palace respectively. The Gushui River was the important source of water for the imperial gardens at that time and eventually flowed into the Luoshui River. In the south of the city, the Yishui River divided into two branches and flowed northward into Waiguocheng. They merged in the city and flowed eastward through the city into the Nanyun Channel, which was an important part of the domestic water and grain transport for the southeast of Luoyang City in the Sui Dynasty. The Chanshui River was at the north of the Luoshui River and flowed southward into the Caoqu Channel.

The artificial water system is mainly composed of the Caoqu Channel, the Xiecheng Channel and the Xiekou Channel. The Caoqu Channel is connected to the Luoshui River, the Chanshui River and the Xiecheng Channel, and eventually flowed into the Luoshui Channel. The Caoqu Channel was the lifeline connecting Luoyang City of the Sui and Tang dynasties to the Grand Canal, and it was also the main traffic artery. The Xiecheng Channel entered the city from the north, connecting with Hanjiacang City and the Caoqu Channel. The Xiekou Channel was an artificial waterway connecting the Xiecheng Channel with the Caoqu Channel.

The Luoyang water system made use of a number of natural and artificial water systems to form a network of water system, and adopted the water system planning with the Luoshui River as the main stream, while other water systems merged into the Luoshui River and flowed into the Yellow River, forming a very distinctive urban water conservancy system. The Luoshui River flowed through the city, which opened up a new era in the construction of the ancient capital of China, and laid a foundation for the water system going through the capital city of Kaifeng and Beijing in later generations.

2. 开封

开封是水陆都会，素有"北方水城"之美誉，境内河流众多，金水河、五丈河（广济渠）、蔡河、汴河（宋代对通济渠的称呼）等四条河流穿城而过，分别通往江南、山东和河南中部，航运十分便捷，各方物资源源不断集中到开封城里。特别是汴河更加重要，《宋史·河渠志》中记载汴河是"横亘中国，首承（大河），漕引江湖，利尽南海，半天下之财赋，并山泽之百货，悉由此路而进"。由此可知，北宋时期不仅江南，而且远至南海的物资都由此水路运到开封，所覆盖的范围已占宋代领土的一半左右。开封由于位居华北，是南来北往的陆路中心，陆上交通也很方便。

在北宋，开封人口众多，约百万人以上。商业极其繁荣，有两万多户人家以经商为业，仅在政府登记的店铺就达 6400 多户，资产十万以上者比比皆是，最多可达百万。此外，还有许多集中的贸易市场。饮食服务行业尤为发达，各种各样的酒楼、饮食店、茶坊鳞次栉比。开封的手工业也极其繁荣，门类众多，军器、瓷器、织锦、印刷、酿酒和刺绣一向闻名，在全国占有重要地位。工人人数也为以前历代首都所不及，仅官营手工业作坊的工匠就达八万人以上。

汴河是北宋国家漕运的重要交通枢纽、商业交通要道。北宋画家张择端画的《清明上河图》，全图大致分为汴京郊外春光、汴河场景、城内街市三部分，纵 24.8 厘米，横 528.7 厘米，绢本淡设色，作品以长卷形式，采用散点透视构图法真实地描绘了当时汴河上交通运输繁忙的景象，再现了 12 世纪北宋全盛时期都城汴京的生活面貌，也是宋代风俗画的最高成就。

张择端在《清明上河图》中，描绘了汴河上漕船运粮的繁忙景象，汴河上穿梭往来的船只，证明了汴京的繁华。从画面上可以看到人烟稠密，粮船云集，人们有在茶馆休息的，有在看相算命的，有在饭铺进餐的；还有"王家纸马店"，是卖扫墓祭品的。河里船只往来，首尾相接，

The opening of the Sui-Tang Grand Canal facilitated the transportation in Luoyang. Together with the Silk Road, the two arteries intersected at Luoyang, one connecting the north and the south, one connecting the west and the east. The Luoyang City became a bustling commercial city, leading to its economic and commercial prosperity, making Luoyang the nation's largest commercial city and a well-known commercial city in the world. The prosperity of commerce also promoted the cultural exchange and integration between the north and the south, which created the unique Heluo culture.

After the Anshi Rebellion in the middle of the Tang Dynasty, Luoyang was seriously damaged and less than 10 percent of the buildings were remained. The city began to decline. Although the Later Liang, the Later Tang and the Later Jin (about less than two years) were established here in the Five Dynasties Period, it still got worse. During the Northern Song Dynasty, Luoyang recovered once and became the academic and cultural center of the Song Dynasty. But after the fall of the Northern Song Dynasty, Luoyang gradually waned.

2. Kaifeng

Kaifeng was a metropolitan by water and land, known as "the Water City of North China". There were many rivers, such as the Jinshui River, the Wuzhang River (the Guangji Channel), the Caihe River and the Bianhe River (the Tongji Channel), so shipping was very convenient, with various goods and materials flowing into Kaifeng. In particular, the Bianhe River was more important than any others. According to *The Records of Rivers and Channels in the History of the Song Dynasty*, the Bianhe River was flowing across China, hundreds of thousands of tons of cargos were transported from the River every year. In the Northern Song Dynasty, supplies from the south of the Yangtze River as well as the South China Sea were transported to Kaifeng by the River, which covered about half of the territory of the Song Dynasty. In addition, Kaifeng, located in North China, was the land route center from the north to the south, so land transportation was very convenient as well.

In the Northern Song Dynasty, Kaifeng had a large population of over one million. Commerce was extremely prosperous, with more than 20,000 businesses and more than 6,400 shops registered in the government. In addition, there were

第三章　运河文化形态

清明上河图局部
Part of *Riverside Scene at Qingming Festival*

或纤夫牵拉，或船夫摇橹，有的满载货物，逆流而上；有的靠岸停泊，正紧张地卸货。横跨汴河上的是一座规模宏大的木质拱桥，它结构精巧，形式优美，宛如飞虹，故名虹桥。有一只大船正待过桥，船夫们有用竹竿撑的，有用长竿钩住桥梁的，有用麻绳挽住船的，还有几人忙着放下

many concentrated trading markets. Catering industry was particularly developed, with a variety of restaurants and tea houses spreading everywhere. Kaifeng's handicraft industry was especially prosperous, and military ware, porcelain, brocade, printing, brewing and embroidery had always been famous, occupying an important position in the whole country. The number of workers outnumbered that of the capitals in previous dynasties, and the number of craftsmen in the official handicraft workshops alone reached more than 80,000.

桅杆，以便船只通过。邻船的人也在指指点点地像在大声吆喝着什么。船里船外都在为此船过桥而忙碌着。桥上的人，也伸头探脑地在为过船的紧张情景捏一把汗。这里是闻名遐迩的虹桥码头区，车水马龙，熙熙攘攘，名副其实是一个水陆交通的会合点。

开封在唐代末年被称为汴州，是五代梁、晋、汉、周的都城。北宋统一，仍建都于此。开封也称为汴京或者东京（另有西京洛阳、北京大名、南京商丘），这里离江南鱼米之乡比较近，大运河的作用就更为明显了。北宋定都汴京，一个重要原因就是汴京有一条汴河沟通南北，这条汴河能够方便地通过漕运把各地的粮食运送到汴京，这促使了汴京的繁华。汴河是开封赖以建都的生命线，也是东南物资漕运东京的大动脉，不仅对京城有重要作用，而且还保证了北方边疆军事上的需要。不仅江淮、荆湖、两浙、福建，而且远至四川、两广的漕运物资，也都在真（今江苏仪征）、扬（今江苏扬州）、楚（今江苏淮安）、泗州改装纲船，经汴河运送京师。北宋时期，长年穿梭在汴河从事漕运的船只多达6000艘。每年通过大运河由江南运到开封的粮食，一般都在500万～600万石，最多的时候达到800万石，大大超过唐代的漕运量。由于汴河沿线往来舟船、客商络绎不绝，临河自然形成众多被称为"河市"的交易场所，其中东京（今开封）河段的河市最为繁华。

3. 郑州

很多人知道今天的郑州是火车拉来的城市，是重要的铁路交通枢纽。其实古代郑州是漕运的中心，水陆交通便利。如果在中国地图上将隋唐大运河按照历史记载标注出来，会形成一个巨大的"人"字，而郑州就是它的中心所在。运河对郑州的城市发展影响非常大，当时郑州号称全国八大雄州之一，既是运河的码头，又是陆路的驿站，是南北物资贸易、文化交流的枢纽。驿站彻夜不关城门，来来往往的商旅、信使络绎不绝。

郑州大运河属于隋唐大运河通济渠段，自偃师与郑州市巩义交界处

The Bianhe River was an important transportation hub and commercial traffic artery in the Northern Song Dynasty. The painting *Riverside Scene at Qingming Festival* by Zhang Zeduan, the painter in the Northern Song Dynasty, can be roughly divided into three parts, including spring scenery outside Bianjing, the scene of the Bianhe River and the streets inside the city. The painting, 528.7 centimeters long, 24.8 centimeters wide, vividly depicts the busy scene on the Bianhe River at that time, and recreates the real life of Bianjing (now Kaifeng), the capital of the Northern Song Dynasty in its heyday in the twelfth century. It is the highest achievement of genre painting in the Song Dynasty.

In *Riverside Scene at Qingming Festival*, Zhang Zeduan described the busy scene of the grain transport on the Bianhe River. The barges passing through the River proved the prosperity of the Bianjing City. On the painting some are having a rest in the teahouse, some talking with a fortune-teller, some having a meal in the restaurant, while others busy on the barges or around the barges. In addition, across the Bianhe River is a large-scale wooden arch bridge, which has an exquisite structure, like a flying rainbow, so it was named Hongqiao. The famous Hongqiao Dockland, bustling with traffic, is where the land and water transportation meets.

Kaifeng, called Bianzhou in the late Tang Dynasty, was the capital of Liang, Jin, Han and Zhou in the Five Dynasties Period. When the Northern Song Dynasty was unified, its capital was also built here and was called Bianjing or Dongjing. It is close to the land of fish and rice in the south of the Yangtze River, so the Grand Canal was becoming increasingly important. One of the important reasons for Bianjing being the capital of the Northern Song Dynasty was that the Bianhe River in Bianjing connected the north and the south, which could carry the grain across the country to Bianjing, thus promoting the prosperity of Bianjing. The Bianhe River was not only the lifeline of Kaifeng, but also the main artery of materials transported to Dongjing from the southeast, which not only was particularly important to the capital, but also ensured the military needs in the northern border. Grain transportation supplies from Zhejiang, Fujian, Sichuan, Guangzhou and Guangxi were also transported by ship in Jiangsu and transported to Bianjing via the Bianhe River. During the Northern Song Dynasty, there were as many as 6,000 vessels transported to and from the Bianhe River all the year round. Every year, the grain transported by the Grand Canal from the regions in the South of the Yangtze

入境，经巩义市、荥阳市、惠济区、金水区、中牟县，东南与开封县境相接，全长150余公里，文化遗产共3项6处，即汴河故道郑州段（通济渠荥阳故城段）、惠济桥、荥阳故城。大运河通济渠段主要位于郑州市惠济区北部，现今河道被称为索须河，西起惠济区北部的丰硕桥，向东在祥云寺村汇入贾鲁河，全长约15公里。其引黄河水的一段河道，北起黄河南岸惠济区北部牛庄大王庙，流经惠济桥、铁炉寨村，在堤湾村注入通济渠后东折。现存地面上的通济渠郑州段河床宽200~300米不等，河堤宽20余米，顶宽7米，河面宽40~70米不等。由于历史

今贾鲁河
Today's Jialu River

River to Kaifeng was 5 to 6 million dan, and the maximum was 8 million dan, which enormously exceeded the grain transported in the Tang Dynasty. Due to the continuous flow of boats and merchants along the Bianhe River, many trading places called "Market on Water" came into being, among which the market in the section of Dongjing was the most prosperous.

3. Zhengzhou

Zhengzhou, as many people know today, is an important railway transportation hub. In ancient times, Zhengzhou was the center of grain transport, with convenient land and water transportation. If the Sui-Tang Grand Canal was marked on a Chinese map in accordance with historical records, it would form a huge letter "Y", and Zhengzhou was just at its center. The Canal had a great influence on the urban development of Zhengzhou. At that time, Zhengzhou was known as one of the eight great regions in China. It was not only the wharf of the Grand Canal and the courier station on land, but also the hub of material trade and cultural exchange between the north and the south. The courier stations were open all night, with endless streams of merchants and messengers coming in and out.

Zhengzhou Grand Canal belonged to the Tongji section of the Sui-Tang Grand Canal, stretching from Gongyi County to Kaifeng County, with a length of more than 150 kilometers and 6 cultural heritage sites. The Tongji section of the Grand Canal was mainly located in the north of Huiji District, Zhengzhou City. It is now known as the Suoxu River, starting from the Fengshuo Bridge in the north of Huiji District in the west, and joining the Jialu River in the east at Xiangyun Temple Village, with a total length of about 15 kilometers. The section of the channel leading to the Yellow River starts from the King Temple of Niuzhuang in the north of Huiji District on the south bank of the Yellow River, flows through Huiji Bridge and Tieluzhai Village, and then flows into the Tongji Channel in the east in the Diwan Village, and then flows eastward. The existing riverbed in Zhengzhou section of the Tongji Channel varies in width from 200 to 300 meters, with the river surface 40 to 70 meters wide. The riverbank is more than 20 meters wide, with the top 7 meters wide. In history, the Yellow River has changed its course many times and the ancient Canal was submerged several times, too. The channel that led the Yellow River into the Canal has been buried

上黄河多次变道,数次湮没运河古道,引黄河水入渠的河段河道已经深埋于地下,只有现存南部的通济渠荥阳故城河段仍存于地表并发挥着泄洪排涝作用。

郑州市惠济区也因境内遗存通济渠的惠济长桥而得名,境内有西山遗址、古荥汉代冶铁遗址和荥阳故城等 3 处全国重点文物保护单位。从西山遗址至今,荥泽古城见证了华夏文明 5000 多年的悠久历史。5300 年前,西山仰韶文化晚期城在黄河边建成,黄帝曾经在此生活;春秋时期,晋文公在此筑践土会天下诸侯;2200 年前,古城因楚河汉界——鸿沟而闻名天下,成为中国名郡;隋朝,隋炀帝以东都为中心开通大运河,第一次连通华夏东西南北,维护了中国的统一稳定,促进了中国的经济发展,造就了唐宋的辉煌与巅峰。

中国大运河通济渠郑州段历史悠久,是中国北方地区最早的、沟通黄河与淮河两大水系的运河遗存,其历史可以追溯至公元前 360 年魏惠王开凿的鸿沟水道,是中国开凿较早的运河之一,也是中国古代最早的黄淮平原上沟通黄河与济、汝、淮、泗诸河的水道交通网。隋代时中国大运河通济渠郑州段是通济渠的渠首,后经唐、宋王朝不断地疏浚维护,全段发挥作用直到金元之际。中国大运河通济渠郑州段经历了 1500 多年的沧桑风雨,反映了中国运河鼎盛时期的状况,是中国大运河的杰出代表。此后,元、明、清时期疏浚的贾鲁河等河流多利用运河故道,也是中国北方地区自战国至今 2000 多年运河开发利用史的见证。

deep underground. Only the existing ancient city section of Xingyang of the Tongji Channel in the south remains on the surface and plays the role of flood discharge and waterlogging drainage.

The Huiji District of Zhengzhou City was also named after the ruins of Huiji Bridge over the Tongji Channel. Within its territory there are three national key cultural relics protection units, such as Xishan Mountain Ruins, Iron Melting Site of the Han Dynasty in Guxing Town and Ancient Town of Xingyang. From the Xishan Mountain Ruins, the ancient city of Xingze has witnessed a 5,000-year history of Chinese civilization. 5,300 years ago, the city of the late Yangshao culture in Xishan was built near the Yellow River, where Yellow Emperor once lived. In the Spring and Autumn Period, Duke Wen of Jin held an association here to meet the governors and kings of Ducal states. 2,200 years ago, the city became famous for the Honggou Canal, the boundary between Chu and Han, and became a famous county in China. In the Sui Dynasty, with Dongdu as the center, Emperor Yang opened the Grand Canal. For the first time, China was connected in all directions, which maintained the unification and stability of the Chinese nation, promoted the economic development of the Chinese nation, and created the glory and peak of the Tang and Song dynasties.

The Zhengzhou section of the Tongji Channel is the earliest canal ruins connecting the Yellow River and the Huaihe River in northern China. Its history can be traced back to the Honggou Channel dug in 360 BC by King Hui of Wei, which is one of the earliest canal in China and ancient China's earliest waterway transportation network on the Huanghuai Plains to connect the Yellow River and the Jihe River, the Ruhe River, the Huaihe River, the Sizhuhe River, etc. In the Sui Dynasty, Zhengzhou section of the Tongji Channel, an outstanding representative of the Grand Canal, was the canal head of the Tongji Channel. After continuous dredging and maintenance in the Tang and Song dynasties, the whole Canal played its role until the Jin and Yuan dynasties, experiencing more than 1,500 years of vicissitudes, reflecting the situation of the heyday of the Grand Canal. Since then, the Jialu River and other rivers dredged in the Yuan, Ming and Qing dynasties also used the old canal route, which witnesses the history of the Canal development and utilization of northern China for more than 2,000 years since the Warring States Period.

二、运河城镇

　　由河南大运河的流动与城镇经贸往来，兴起了卫辉古城、山阳古城、浚县古城、卫国故城、滑县道口古镇、开封朱仙镇、中牟万胜镇、南乐元村古镇等一批中原文化名城（镇），形成运河城镇文化品牌。运河古城镇是古往今来商贸交易与文化交流的中转站、集聚地，是农耕文明与商业文明的产物，是保存大运河历史记忆的地标性符号。

1. 浚县古城

　　浚县位于河南北部鹤壁市境内，地处太行山与华北平原过渡地带，是河南省唯一的县级国家历史文化名城。境内有名胜古迹300多处，古城内的大运河浚县段、黎阳仓遗址被列入中国大运河世界文化遗产。

黎阳仓遗址
Ancient site of Liyang Granary

　　河南大运河浚县段的卫河自浚县新镇镇入境，流经新镇镇、小河镇、

II. The Towns along the Canal

With the strengthening of economic and trade exchanges between the towns in Henan along the Grand Canal, a number of famous cultural ancient towns have emerged in the Central Plains, such as Weihui, Shanyang, Xunxian, Weiguo, Daokou in Huaxian County, Zhuxianzhen in Kaifeng, Wansheng in Zhongmu, and Yuancun in Nanle County, thus forming the urban culture of the Grand Canal towns. As the products of the interaction between agricultural civilization and commercial civilization, the ancient canal towns are the gathering places and transit stations for business and cultural exchanges through the ages and have become the landmarks which preserve the historical memory of the Grand Canal.

1. Xunxian Ancient Town

Xunxian County, located in Hebi City, northern Henan Province and in the transitional zone between Taihang Mountain and North China Plain, is the only county-level national historical and cultural town in Henan Province. There are more than 300 scenic spots and historical sites in Xunxian County, including Xunxian section of the Grand Canal and Liyang Granary Site, both of which are listed as World Cultural Heritage.

Weihe River in Xunxian section of Henan Grand Canal enters Xunxian from Xinzhen, flows through towns of Xinzhen, Xiaohe, Liyang, Chengguan, Tunzi and Wangzhuang, runs through Xunxian County from north to south, with a total length of 71.1 kilometers, and is composed of many tributaries, such as Qihe River and Tanghe River. More than 1,800 years ago, for military needs, Cao Cao, a Chinese warlord and statesman of the Three Kingdoms Period, ordered to block the Qihe River in the southwest of Xunxian County and divert water to Baigou, the old course of the Yellow River, which made the Qihe River separated from the Yellow River. The Baigou Waterway Project built by Cao Cao laid the foundation for Emperor Yang of Sui to open the Yongji Channel.

More than 1,400 years ago Liyang Granary along the Grand Canal was an important granary of the central government during the Sui and Tang dynasties. After archaeological exploration, the researchers found that the main relics related

黎阳镇、城关镇、屯子镇、王庄乡6个乡镇，贯穿浚县南北，全长71.1公里，由淇河、汤河等多条支流汇集而成。1800多年前，一代枭雄曹操为了军事上的需要，在浚县西南部截留了淇河水并引入白沟，从而使淇河脱离黄河，流入了黄河故道白沟。曹操创修的白沟水运工程为后来隋炀帝开通永济渠打下了基础。

距今1400多年的黎阳仓是隋唐时期大运河沿岸重要的国家官署粮仓。经过考古勘探，工作人员发现了与黎阳仓有关的主要遗迹有仓城的城墙、护城河、仓窖、夯土台基、大型建筑基址、路、墓葬、灰坑等。这座依山而建的古粮仓，总储量达到了3360万斤，可供8万人吃1年，所以有"黎阳收，顾九州"的美誉。

浚县古庙会是浚县古城的重要民俗。浚县正月古庙会起源于后赵皇帝石勒开凿伾山大佛时期，周围群众集结进香、朝山拜佛，盛时会首20余名，会众640人。宋代以来，浚县两山相继修筑了许多寺庙和道观，庙会规模逐渐扩大。至明嘉靖二十一年（1542年），浮丘山碧霞宫的建成令浚县古庙会有了基本规模。浚县古庙会与山东泰山庙会、山西白云山庙会、北京妙峰山庙会并称华北地区四大庙会。

浚县古庙会是集民间艺术、民间信仰、物资交流、文化娱乐为一体的民俗娱乐活动。会期从农历正月初一到二月二长达一个月，其中正月十五、十六举行民间艺术巡展盛会，有三层人叠起的高跷、太师椅上高空翻滚的舞狮、盘鼓、秧歌、旱船等丰富多彩的民间文艺表演活动以及中原民间工艺精品展、祈福大法会、元宵节吉祥灯会等，充分展示浚县以村镇为单位的民间的民俗表演节目。表演队伍穿过县城到会场，从大伾东山大佛到浮丘西山的云霞仙子延绵近十里。浚县古庙会保持着明清特色，吸引着周边省市以及海内外的数百万香客游人。庙会期间每天从周边各地来这里的观光游览者多达几万人，高峰期有50多万人。为此，浚县古庙会被列入河南民俗经典、首批河南"老字号"、首批河南古代暨近代民居民间建筑保护名录。

to the Liyang Granary include the city walls, moats, warehouse cellars, rammed earth foundations, foundations of large buildings, roads, tombs, ash pits and so on. This ancient granary, built at the foot of the mountain, had a total reserve of 33.6 million catties, which could feed 80,000 people for one year. Therefore, it enjoyed a high reputation of "the harvest in Liyang heralds the prosperity of the country".

Xunxian Temple Fair is an important folk custom of Xunxian ancient town. It originated from the period when Emperor Shile of the Latter Zhao Dynasty built the Big Buddha in Pishan Mountain. At that time, the surrounding people gathered for pilgrimages and worshiped Buddha in the mountains. In its heyday, there were more than 20 leaders and 640 members of the congregation. Since the Song Dynasty, many temples and Taoist temples have been built in the two mountains of Xunxian County, and the scale of the Temple Fair has gradually expanded. In the twenty-first year of Jiajing in the Ming Dynasty (1542), the completion of Bixia Palace in Fuqiu Mountain made Xunxian Temple Fair have a basic scale. Xunxian Temple Fair, Shandong Taishan Temple Fair, Shanxi Baiyunshan Temple Fair and Beijing Miaofengshan Temple Fair are called the four major temple fairs in North China.

Xunxian Temple Fair is a folk entertainment activity integrating folk art, folk belief, material exchange and cultural entertainment. The meeting lasted for one month from the first day of the first month of the lunar calendar to the second day of the second month. In the grand folk art exhibition held on the fifteenth and sixteenth days of the first month, there were colorful folk art performances, such as stilts folded by three people, lion dance, drum, yangko, land boat and so on, as well as the Central Plains folk arts and crafts exhibition, the Blessing Buddhist Fair and the lantern show of the Lantern Festival, which fully demonstrated the folk performances of villages and towns in Xunxian County. The performance team traveled through the county to the venue, stretching for nearly ten miles from the Big Buddha of Dapi Mountain to Yunxia Fairy in Fuqiu Mountain. Xunxian Temple Fair maintains the characteristics of temple fairs in Ming and Qing dynasties, attracting millions of pilgrims from surrounding provinces and cities as well as from home and abroad. Every day, tens of thousands of tourists come here for sightseeing, with more than 500,000 people at the peak. Therefore, Xunxian Temple Fair was listed in the Henan Folk Custom Classics, the first

浚县古城墙
Ancient City Wall of Xunxian County

2. 道口古镇

道口镇坐落在河南省滑县西北部的卫河之滨，是中国历史文化名镇。中国大运河永济渠卫河段从道口古镇穿城而过，现存有原生态的古河道、古码头、古城墙、古庙宇、古民居、古商号等丰富的历史遗存，共有各类历史建筑 2000 多间，见证了大运河的千年繁华。

道口古镇就是今天道口镇顺河古街一带的老街，沿卫河而建，因大运河而兴。道口古镇最先建于黄河西岸的鲧堤之上，依卫河而兴起。关于"道口"名字的由来，据说是因有李姓人家在黄河渡口摆渡而得名，史称李家道口，距今已有 1000 多年历史。但道口镇真正繁荣始于隋炀帝开凿大运河，由于永济渠卫河段流经这里，道口镇成了远近闻名的码头。

到了明代初年，朱棣迁都北京，重修大运河，并在道口设递运所运输官资、军需，古镇因此日益繁荣。道口古镇依靠大运河航运，上达辉县（今辉县市）百泉，下抵天津，交通顺畅，航运发达。明清时期，道

batch of Henan "Time-Honored Brands", and the first batch of Henan Ancient and Modern Residential Building Protection List.

2. Daokou Ancient Town

Daokou is located on the shore of Weihe River in the northwest of Huaxian County, Henan Province. It is a famous historical and cultural town in China. The Weihe River section of the Yongji Channel of China Grand Canal passes through the ancient town. There are abundant historical relics in the town, such as ancient rivers, ancient docks, ancient city walls, ancient temples, ancient dwellings, and ancient trade houses. There are more than 2,000 historical buildings of various types, which have witnessed the thousand-year prosperity of the Grand Canal.

Daokou, which originated from Shunhe Ancient Street, was built along the Weihe River and flourished because of the Grand Canal. This ancient town was first built on the dike on the west bank of the Yellow River, and developed with the construction of the Weihe River. It is said that the name "Daokou" originated from the town's Li family who ferried at the Yellow River ferry, known as Li family's Daokou (ferry) in history. Daokou has a history of more than 1,000 years. Its real prosperity began with Emperor Yang of Sui ordering to dig the Grand Canal, and Daokou became a well-known wharf because the Weihe River section of the Yongji Channel flowed through here.

In the early years of the Ming Dynasty, Zhu Di moved his capital to Beijing, rebuilt the Grand Canal, and set up a delivery station in Daokou to transport official assets and military supplies, which made the ancient town increasingly prosperous. Daokou Ancient Town relied on the Grand Canal for shipping, reaching Baiquan in Huixian County (present-day Huixian City) in the south and arriving in Tianjin in the north, with smooth traffic and developed shipping. During the Ming and Qing dynasties, the land and water transportation in Daokou was so developed that many merchants gathered here to do business. During the period of the Republic of China, Daokou, Zhuxianzhen, Shedian and Zhoukou were called "Four Famous Towns in the Central Plains". In the late Qing Dynasty, the ancient town entered its heyday. As a result of the completion of Daoqing Railway in 1907, it became a "land and water terminal" connecting railways, highways, and waterways, and its transportation network extended in all

口镇可以说是水陆交通发达，商贾云集，货物鳞次栉比。在民国年间，道口镇与朱仙镇、赊店、周口并称"中原四大名镇"。而道口古镇最鼎盛的晚清时期，由于1907年道清铁路的修通，这里成了连接铁路、公路、航运的"水旱码头"，交通网四通八达，素有"千年古镇小天津"之誉。

在道口镇的物产中，道口烧鸡是道口古镇名扬四海的中原美食，被誉为"中州名馐"。道口烧鸡创始于清顺治十八年（1661年），距今已有300多年的历史。据当地县志记载，在开始的100多年时间里，由于技术条件差，还没有什么起色，生意并不兴隆。到乾隆五十二年（1787年），张氏的先祖张炳，一次在大街上闲逛，偶遇一位曾在清宫御膳房做过厨师的刘义。刘义为感谢当年张家救济恩情，将宫廷烧鸡秘方无偿传授给张炳。张炳从此得"要想烧鸡香，八料加老汤"的秘诀。八料即为陈皮、肉桂、豆蔻、白芷、丁香、草果、砂仁和良姜等八种佐料，张炳按其用法、用量，依法烹制，制作出"色、香、味、烂"等俱佳的烧鸡。从此，张炳的烧鸡生意越做越兴隆，张炳就取了刘义的"义"和他们的"张"姓，把店铺取名"义兴张"。张炳家族的烧鸡声誉大振，远近闻名，并定铺号名为"义兴张"。

从此以后，人们所说的道口烧鸡，其实主要就是"义兴张"的烧鸡。20世纪50年代，义兴张第六代传人张和礼公开了祖传的烧鸡秘方。从此以后义兴张烧鸡制作技艺就没有了秘密，义兴张也就成了全道口乃至全国的义兴张。今天的道口古镇大集街的街口，还有一家"义兴张"的烧鸡老店，里面俨然就是一个小型的道口烧鸡博物馆。

名扬四方的道口烧鸡、驰名海外的道口锡器、盛极一时的同和裕银号、镖局镖师流传下来的武术功夫……无不记录着古镇的昔日辉煌。民居、商号、码头、寨墙见证了古镇千年的繁华。大运河申遗成功前后，道口镇多方筹集资金6000多万元，集中开展了河道、城墙、码头等文物本体维修和环境整治、河道清淤等工作。道口镇也先后建成了古镇民俗展馆、同和裕银号展馆、运河历史文化展馆与大运河非物质文化遗产

directions, so it has been long reputed as small Tianjin (a big coastal city in North China).

Among the specialties of Daokou, Roast Chicken, known as "Zhongzhou Famous Cuisine", is famous all over the world. Daokou Roast Chicken started in the eighteenth year of Shunzhi in the Qing Dynasty (1661) and has a history of more than 300 years. According to Daokou's county annals, in the first 100 years, due to the poor cooking skills, Daokou Roast Chicken was not famous at all. In the fifty-second year of the Qianlong (1787), Zhang Bing, the ancestor of Zhang's family, once strolled in the street and met Liu Yi, who had worked as a chef in the imperial dining room of the Qing Dynasty. In order to repay the Zhang family for their kindness in the past, Liu Yi told Zhang Bing the secret recipe of royal roast chicken free of charge. From then on, Zhang Bing got the secret recipe of "If you want to roast fragrant chicken, add eight ingredients to the soup decocted". The eight ingredients are tangerine peel, cinnamon, cardamom, dahurian angelica root, clove, tsaoko, amomum fruit and galangal, etc. According to Liu Yi's recipe, Zhang Bing cooked roast chicken with excellent color, fragrance, taste and softness. Since then, the reputation of the roast chicken of Zhang Bing's family has been greatly enhanced, and the roast chicken business has become more and more prosperous. Zhang Bing named his shop "Yixingzhang" after Liu Yi's "Yi" and Zhang's family name, which means the prosperity of the Zhang family comes from the help of Liu Yi.

Since then, what people call Daokou Roast Chicken is actually the "Yixingzhang" Roast Chicken. In the 1950s, Zhang Heli, the sixth-generation successor of "Yixingzhang", publicized the ancestral secret recipe of roast chicken. Since then, there has been no secret about the production skills of Yixingzhang Roast Chicken, and these skills have spread throughout the entire Daokou and even the whole country. Today, at the corner of Daji Street in Daokou Ancient Town, there is an old "Yixingzhang" Roast Chicken shop, which is just like a small Daokou roast chicken museum.

The well-known Daokou Roast Chicken, the famous Daokou tin ware, the flourishing Tongheyu banking house, and the martial arts skills handed down by the guards of the escort... all record the past glory of the ancient town. Residential houses, business houses, docks, and walls have witnessed the prosperity of the

展示场馆、老粮仓保护性修缮及监测中心，这对于保护和弘扬运河古镇文化起到了积极作用。

义兴张烧鸡铺
"Yixingzhang" Roast Chicken shop

3. 朱仙镇

朱仙镇位于河南省开封市西南部。明清时期，朱仙镇因贾鲁河的开通而走向鼎盛，成为"南船北车"的转运处和货物集散地，与广东佛山镇、江西景德镇、湖北汉口镇同为全国"四大名镇"。

据《祥符县志》记载，朱仙镇原名聚仙镇，后因战国朱亥的食邑和封地而得名。太平兴国九年（984年），宋太宗令"凿尉氏县界新河90里，数旬而毕"，拉直了的新河使朱仙驿因紧邻蔡河而成开封附近的水陆要冲，由村落而成驿站，进而成为集镇。金元时期，随着开封地位的衰落，运河的变迁，以及黄河改道，朱仙镇也就逐渐衰落了。

元朝建都大都（今北京），把大运河改建为南北向，直通京都，河

ancient town for thousands of years. During the period of applying for the World Heritage of the Grand Canal, Daokou Government raised more than 60 million *yuan* from various sources and concentrated on the maintenance of cultural relics such as rivers, city walls and docks, environmental remediation and river dredging. In Daokou, the Ancient Town Folklore Exhibition Hall, Tongheyu Banking House Exhibition Hall, Canal History and Culture Exhibition Hall, Grand Canal Intangible Cultural Heritage Exhibition Hall and Old Granary Protective Renovation and Monitoring Center have been built successively, which have played a positive role in protecting and promoting the ancient canal town's culture.

3. Zhuxianzhen

Zhuxianzhen is located in the southwest of Kaifeng City, Henan Province. During the Ming and Qing dynasties, Zhuxianzhen reached its peak due to the dredging of Jialu River, becoming a transshipment place and cargo distribution center, and being one of the "Four Famous Towns" in China together with Foshan in Guangdong, Jingdezhen in Jiangxi and Hankou in Hubei.

According to *Xiangfu County Annals*, originally named Juxianzhen, Zhuxianzhen was later named after the fief of Zhu Hai in the Warring States Period. In the ninth year of Taipingxingguo (984), Emperor Taizong of Song ordered Xinhe River at the border of Weishi County to be dug for another 45 kilometers. This project was completed in a few months, and the straightened Xinhe River made Zhuxian Posthouse become a water and land hub near Kaifeng because it adjoined the Caihe River. So, this area changed from a village to a posthouse, and then became a market town. During the Jin and Yuan dynasties, with the decline of Kaifeng, the change of the Canal and the diversion of the Yellow River, Zhuxianzhen was on the wane.

In the Yuan Dynasty, Dadu (present-day Beijing) was set as the capital, and the Grand Canal was rebuilt to the north-south direction, leading directly to the capital. Therefore, the water transportation of the Bianqu Canal in Henan was gradually abandoned. At that time the Yellow River flooded and burst frequently, which happened in the 40 years of the 95 years from the ninth year of Zhiyuan (1272) to the twenty-sixth year of Zhizheng (1366) and sometimes, in just one year, the Yellow River burst in many places. According to records, in the first year

朱仙镇启封故园

Qifeng Garden in Zhuxianzhen

南汴渠漕运逐渐废弃。元代黄河决溢频繁，自至元九年（1272年）到至正二十六年（1366年）的95年中，就决溢40年，有时一年就决口十几处或几十处。随后，几乎年年决溢。据记载，自宋端平元年（金天兴三年，1234年）蒙古军在开封以北寸金淀决河以灌宋军以后，黄河可能由封丘南、开封东至陈留、杞县分为三股：一股经鹿邑、亳州等地会涡水入淮；一股经归德（今商丘）、徐州，合泗水故道南下入淮；一股由杞县、太康，经陈州会颍水至颍州南入淮。至元二十三年（1286年），"河决开封、祥符、陈留、杞（县）、太康、通许、鄢陵、扶沟、洧川、

in Duanping in the Song Dynasty (the third year of Tianxing in the Jin Dynasty, 1234), the Mongolian army dug the Yellow River levee in Cunjindian, north of Kaifeng, to drown the Song army. Since then, the Yellow River has been divided into three branches from the south of Fengqiu and the east of Kaifeng to Chenliu and Qixian: the first one flows into the Wo River and then into the Huaihe River via Luyi and Bozhou; the second one flows into the old channel of the Sishui River via Guide (now Shangqiu) and Xuzhou, and then flows into the Huaihe River in the south; the third one flows into the Yinghe River from Qixian County, Taikang County and Chenzhou, and then flows into the Huaihe River from Yingzhou. In the twenty-third year of Zhiyuan (1286), the Yellow River burst in Kaifeng, Xiangfu, Chenliu, Qixian, Taikang, Tongxu, Yanling, Fugou, Weichuan, Weishi, Yangwu, Yanjin, Zhongmu, Yuanwu (now Yuanyang County) and Suizhou. In the first year of Dade in the Yuan Dynasty (1297), the Yellow River burst in Pukou, Qixian County, and flooded for 200 miles. The flood flowed to the horizontal dike of Guide (now Shangqiu) and into the Huaihe River together with the ancient Bianhe River. In the fourth year of Zhizheng (1344), the Yellow River burst at Baimaokou (now Cao County, Shandong Province) and flooded for seven years. Only in April of the eleventh year of Zhizheng (1351) did the court send Jia Lu to control the flood. The scale of Jia Lu's project of blocking flooding is rare in the history of river management in feudal times. Jia Lu's flood control project not only eliminated the flood, but also revived the water transportation, so the dredged channel was named the Jialu River. After that, Zhuxianzhen, as the shipping destination of the Jialu River and the only outer port of Kaifeng, became an indispensable part of this city.

Jia Lu was a famous flood control official in the Yuan Dynasty, and also an excellent water conservancy expert in harnessing the Yellow River. After being appointed as the Water Superintendent, Jia Lu made field investigations along the River, went back and forth thousands of miles, obtained first-hand information on flood control, and presented a drawing report to the court. Jia Lu put forward two river harnessing schemes: one was to build a dike on the north bank of the new channel downstream of the breach to limit the cross-flow of floods, and this scheme had a small amount of engineering; the other was to block the breach and dredge the downstream river channel, thus leading the water back to the old

尉氏、阳武、延津、中牟、原武（今原阳县）、睢州15处"。元大德元年（1297年），黄河在杞县蒲口决口，黄水直趋200里，至归德（今商丘）横堤以下和古汴水合流入淮河。至正四年（1344年），黄河在白茅口（今山东省曹县境内）决口，泛滥7年，到至正十一年（1351年）四月，朝廷才派贾鲁治河。贾鲁堵口工程规模之浩大，为封建时代治河史上所罕见。贾鲁治河既消除了水患，又复兴了漕运，所疏通的这条河道被命名为贾鲁河。贾鲁河开通之后朱仙镇作为贾鲁河航运终点，成为开封唯一的外港，是开封不可或缺的重要组成部分。

贾鲁是元代著名的河防大臣，也是一位在治理黄河上卓有成效的水利专家。在受命为行都水监使后，贾鲁就沿河道实地考察，往返数千里不辞劳苦，取得治河第一手资料，并向朝廷进献绘图报告，提出两个治河方案：一是就决口以下新河道北岸筑堤，限制决河横流，工程量小；一是堵塞决口，同时疏浚下游河道，挽河回故道，这是事半功倍的做法。至正十一年（1351年），55岁的贾鲁出任工部尚书兼总治河防使，指挥15万民夫和2万士兵，开始了黄河治理史上这场著名的"贾鲁治河"。

朱仙镇木版年画是中国古老的传统工艺品之一，被列入第一批国家级非物质文化遗产名录。朱仙镇年画源于汉唐壁画艺术，题材和内容大多取自历史戏剧、演义小说、神话故事和民间传说，融入了中原文化的审美观念和崇神意识，反映了农民希冀五谷丰登、富裕兴旺、和睦如意、平安吉祥、六畜兴旺等美好的生活愿望，以及扶正祛邪、爱憎分明的思想感情，具有独特的地方色彩和淳朴古老的民族风格。北宋年间，汴京作为全国政治、经济、文化中心，活跃的世俗文艺给年画的创作提供了丰厚的土壤。在这一时期，雕版印刷技术的成熟，使供不应求的笔绘年画转向刻印年画，并且官办与民办作坊齐开，使开封木版年画的印刷及销售盛况空前，很快影响到全国。在反映北宋开封百姓生活状况的《东京梦华录》中，谈到了在市井中人们印制和售卖以门神、钟馗为内容的年画。可见朱仙镇年画在北宋时期已逐渐成熟。

channel, which can get twice the result with half the effort. In the eleventh year of Zhizheng (1351), 55-year-old Jia Lu took up the posts of Minister of Industry and Trade and General Flood Prevention Officer, commanding 150,000 workers and 20,000 soldiers, and started the famous project of "Jia Lu Controlling Flood" in the history of the Yellow River regulation.

The Zhuxianzhen Woodcut New Year Picture is one of the ancient traditional handicrafts in China, and has been selected into the first batch of National Intangible Cultural Heritage List. Zhuxianzhen New Year pictures originated from mural art in the Han and Tang dynasties. The theme and content are mostly based on historical dramas, novels, myths and folklore. With the unique local characteristics and simple national style, Zhuxianzhen New Year pictures incorporate the aesthetic concept and worship consciousness of Central Plains culture and reflect the farmers' desire for a prosperous, harmonious, and happy life as well as the feeling of pursuing justice and exorcising evil spirits. During the Northern Song Dynasty, Bianjing, as the national political, economic and cultural center, provided the solid foundation for the creation of New Year pictures with active secular literature and art. During this period, with the maturity of engraving printing technology, pen-painted New Year pictures, which were in short supply, turned to engraving New Year pictures, and the government-run and private workshops opened together, which made the printing and sales of Kaifeng Woodcut New Year Pictures unprecedented. Soon Kaifeng Woodcut New Year Pictures quickly became popular throughout the country. *The Eastern Capital: A Dream of Splendor*, which reflects the living conditions of Kaifeng people in the Northern Song Dynasty, describes that people printed and sold New Year pictures with door gods and Zhong Kui (a ghost catcher in Chinese mythology) in the market. It can be seen that the art of Zhuxianzhen Woodcut New Year Pictures had gradually matured in the Northern Song Dynasty.

After the demise of the Northern Song Dynasty, the Song royal family moved south. Some artists from Zhuxianzhen fled to Jiangsu and Zhejiang Provinces in the south and they brought the folk art of woodcut New Year picture there. In order to meet the aesthetic needs of local people, artists developed Taohuawu Woodcut New Year Pictures by using the production skills of Zhuxianzhen Woodcut New Year Pictures and combining with local folk customs. Therefore,

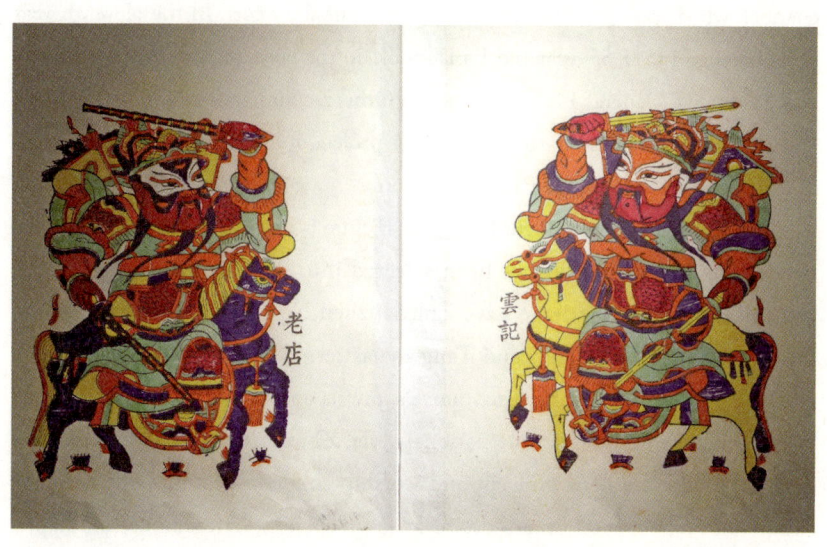

朱仙镇木版年画
Zhuxianzhen Woodcut New Year Pictures

　　北宋灭亡后，宋王室南迁，一部分朱仙镇的艺人逃到南方江浙一带，同时也把这一民间艺术带到了江浙一带。为了迎合当地百姓的审美需求，艺人们运用朱仙镇年画的生产技艺，结合当地民俗民风，发展出新的桃花坞木版年画。桃花坞木版年画和朱仙镇年画可以说是传承关系。据说，山东潍坊年画也是从朱仙镇流传过去的，因为朱仙镇距开封20公里，历朝历代黄河曾经泛滥，朱仙镇屡遭淹没，艺人为了谋生，逃生到山东、河北，就形成山东潍坊年画和河北武强年画。北宋灭亡后，金人把能工巧匠掳掠到北方，所以山西年画、陕西年画基本上也是从朱仙镇传过去的。因此，有专家就说，中国木版年画的龙头和源头就是朱仙镇木版年画。

　　明清时期，朱仙镇河道四通八达，随即成为中原的商业重镇。木版年画在繁荣的商埠迅速恢复，买卖兴隆，声名大振。据载，当时朱仙镇从事这一行业的有300余家。清末时，由于朱仙镇河道阻塞，航道不通，木版年画与其他商业都日趋萧条。

Taohuawu Woodcut New Year Pictures are the inheritance of Zhuxianzhen Woodcut New Year Pictures. It is said that the New Year pictures in Weifang, Shandong Province were also passed down from Zhuxianzhen, which is 20 kilometers away from Kaifeng. In history, the Yellow River flooded Kaifeng many times. In order to make a living, Kaifeng artists escaped to Shandong and Hebei. Later, Shandong Weifang New Year pictures and Hebei Wuqiang New Year pictures gradually developed. After the demise of the Northern Song Dynasty, the Jin people plundered skilled craftsmen to the north, so Shanxi New Year pictures and Shaanxi New Year pictures were basically passed down from Zhuxianzhen. Therefore, some experts declare that the origin of Chinese woodcut New Year pictures is Zhuxianzhen New Year pictures.

In the Ming and Qing dynasties, with the rivers extending in all directions, Zhuxianzhen immediately became a commercial center in the Central Plains. The business of woodcut New Year pictures quickly recovered and prospered in this commercial port, and gained a great reputation. According to records, there were more than 300 workshops engaged in this industry in Zhuxianzhen at that time. At the end of the Qing Dynasty, due to the blockage of the river channel in Zhuxianzhen, the business of woodcut New Year pictures was increasingly depressed.

4. Ancient Town of Yuancun

The Ancient Town of Yuancun is located about 15 kilometers west of Nanle County, Puyang City, Henan Province, where the Grand Canal flows through. During the Northern Wei Dynasty (386-557 AD), local people already built a clay wall around the town. There were four gates in the wall. The east gate was called Yingyang, the south gate Fengle, the west gate Daihe, and the north gate Wangjing, which faced the ferry of the town's pier. It is said that the word "Wangjing" on the north gate comes from the handwriting of Empress Dowager Cixi in the Qing Dynasty. Up to now, the stone plaque on the town gate is still kept in Yuancun, and the inscription time is "Shangsi in the first year of Tongzhi", that is, the third day of March of the lunar calendar in 1862.

The origin of the name "Wangjing" was closely related to the prosperity of Yuancun brought by the Grand Canal. In Xianfeng Period of the Qing Dynasty,

4. 元村古镇

元村古镇位于河南省濮阳市南乐县城西约 15 公里处，是大运河流经的地方。北魏时期，元村古镇就已经修筑了土城。土城有四个城门，东门为"迎阳"，南门叫"丰乐"，西门称"带河"，北门名"望京"，直对着古镇码头的大渡口。据说，北门上那"望京"二字大有来头，是出于清朝慈禧太后的亲笔书写。至今，在元村古镇还保存着这块城门上的石质匾额，题款时间是"同治元年上巳"，即 1862 年的农历三月三日。

关于"望京"门名字的由来，与大运河带来元村古镇繁荣密切相关。在清代咸丰年间，元村古镇已经成了远近闻名的卫河商贸重镇，盐场、煤行、粮栈、布庄、药店、杂货铺等各种行当齐全，在码头、古街、河岸星罗棋布，京津洋货、江西瓷器、苏杭锦缎、江南茶叶、南京团扇等商品琳琅满目。全国各地富商大贾带着家眷，在沿河经商或闲居。当时青纱轿、花帘轿、辇车子，甚至南方的滑竿儿，不时在古镇街头巷陌出现，那阵势不顶半个府城，也顶大半拉县城，素有"元村御河一拐弯儿，顶住南乐半个天儿"的美誉。

居住在卫河南岸和古镇街巷的外地客商家眷，以及随商船来古镇寻谋生计的人们，尤其是来自京津地方的外地人，欣赏着卫河两岸的景色，遥望北方天际，难免思念故乡，生出些许浓浓乡愁来。元村一带自古就有"三月三，回娘家"的习俗，此时正值上巳节日，思乡之情尤为深切，或者想起了大诗人杜甫"三月三日天气新，长安水边多丽人"的诗句。于是，她（他）们便相携登高，遥望京津，大多集中在北门之上，翘首北望，呼唤京都津门的亲人。

相传，有人把此事传到了京城，传入了宫闱。恰巧赶上同治皇帝初登大位，他的生身母慈禧皇太后高兴，听到贴身太监传禀如此动情故事，便提笔写了"望京"两个大字，地方镌刻成石匾，镶嵌在古镇的北门正中，成了一段佳话。美丽的传说随着卫河古镇的繁华一直闪烁在人们的记忆里传承下来。

Yuancun had become a famous commercial center of the Weihe River, with a variety of trades, such as saltworks, coal shops, grain warehouses, cloth shops, pharmacies and grocery stores, which were scattered all over the docks, ancient streets and river banks. The goods here were dazzling, including foreign goods transported from Beijing and Tianjin, Jiangxi porcelain, Suzhou-Hangzhou brocade, Jiangnan tea, Nanjing round fan and so on. Along the river, rich businessmen from all over the country did business or lived in leisure with their families. At that time, the green gauze sedan, the flower curtain sedan, the man-drawn carriage, and even the bamboo sedan chair in the south appeared in the streets and lanes of the ancient town from time to time. So, the prosperity of this small town was almost equal to that of Nanle County.

Merchants, especially those from Beijing and Tianjin, came to Yuancun for a living with their families and lived in the streets on the south bank of the Weihe River. Homesickness was always with them. Sometimes, looking at the northern sky while enjoying the scenery on both sides of the Weihe River, they would miss their hometown. There was a custom of "on the third day of the third month of the lunar calendar, a married woman returns to her mother's home" in Yuancun since ancient times. Shangsi Festival was celebrated on this day. On this festival, people who were far away from home were especially homesick and they always helped each other to climb the north gate, looking ahead at Beijing and Tianjin, and calling for their loved ones.

A legend has it that the stories of Yuancun spread to Beijing. At that time, Emperor Tongzhi just ascended the throne, and his mother, Empress Dowager Cixi, was very happy. When she heard such emotional stories from close-fitting eunuchs, she wrote two Chinese characters, "Wangjing", which meant missing hometown Beijing. These two Chinese characters were later engraved on a stone plaque which was embedded in the center of the north gate of Yuancun. This much-told tale still remains in people's memory with the increasing prosperity of the ancient town.

三、运河文脉

  历尽沧桑的大运河，以其独特的方式记载着中华民族的历史。沿河两岸的民情风俗，组成一幅精彩纷呈的绚丽长卷；随处可见的历史遗迹，则保存了中华民族不断前进的踪影。运河故事，是运河两岸人民生息繁衍的片段集结；运河文化，也是世世代代社会生活的生动再现。千年大运河养育了无数的先民，也记录着运河两岸勤劳的先民们的生活，并向后人讲述发生在运河岸边的故事。大运河是稀缺珍贵的活化文化资源，是中华水文化传承的载体，是流动的文化，是中国传统制度文化、技术文化、社会文化的集合体，是国家的标志性遗产，是中华民族流动的精神家园。保护大运河是运河沿线所有地区的共同责任，要认真"保护好、传承好、利用好"大运河历史文化资源。

  大运河是写在中国大地上的流淌的文化，不仅是精神层面的地域文化，更是中华文明的标志和象征。河南是中华文明的重要发祥地，也是隋唐大运河的源头和核心区域，是大运河河道路线最长、流经古都最多、运河遗产最为丰富的省份，已经发掘的黎阳仓、回洛仓、含嘉仓以及相关河道、河堤、码头、桥梁、水工设施等遗址遗迹，充分体现了大运河河南段遗产类型的多样性，而且彰显了大运河河南段历史文化资源独特的历史地位和突出的文化价值。目前，中国隋唐大运河永济渠（卫河）仍在发挥防洪灌溉和生态景观作用，通济渠洛河段仍是黄河的重要支流。

  与京杭大运河相比，隋唐大运河河南段具有更加深沉而厚重的历史文化底蕴。黄河的多次改道与频繁泛滥，导致隋唐大运河的大部分河段淹没在历史的尘埃之中。甚至在黄河故道的地下六七米深处，不少地方至今仍能找到一些隋唐大运河的文化遗迹。据统计，在大运河流经河南的40个县（市、区）核心区内，就分布有世界文化遗产及遗产点10处、全国重点文物保护单位113处、省级文物保护单位325处。大运河河南

III. The Grand Canal Culture

The Grand Canal, which has experienced many vicissitudes, reflects the history of the Chinese nation in its unique way. The life of the people on both sides of the Canal presents a splendid scroll of folk customs. The historical sites that can be seen everywhere along the Canal preserve the trace of the Chinese nation's continuous progress. The story of the Canal is a collection of fragments of the life of the people along the Canal, and the culture of the Canal is also a vivid representation of social life for generations. The Grand Canal nurtured countless industrious ancestors for thousands of years, recording their lives and telling stories to future generations about what happened along the Canal. As a scarce and precious cultural resource and a sign of Chinese water culture, the Grand Canal reflects an integration of traditional Chinese institutional culture, technical culture and social culture. So, it is a symbolic heritage and a flowing spiritual home of the Chinese nation. The protection of the Grand Canal is the common responsibility of all people along the Canal. The historical and cultural resources of the Grand Canal should be effectively protected, inherited and utilized.

The Grand Canal reflects a flowing culture on the land of China, which is not only a spiritual regional culture, but also a symbol of Chinese civilization. As an important birthplace of Chinese civilization, Henan is the source and core area of the Sui-Tang Grand Canal. It is also the province with the longest Canal, the largest number of ancient capitals and the richest Canal heritage. The excavated historical sites fully reflect the diversity of heritage types and the uniqueness of cultural resources in the Henan section of the Grand Canal, such as Liyang Granary, Huiluo Granary, Hanjia Granary and related canals, banks, wharves, bridges and hydraulic facilities, and it stands important historical status and outstanding cultural value. At present, the Yongji Channel (Weihe River) of the Sui-Tang Grand Canal is still playing the role of flood control, irrigation and ecological landscape, and the Luohe River section of the Tongji Channel is still an important tributary of the Yellow River.

Compared with the Beijing-Hangzhou Grand Canal, the Henan section of the Sui-Tang Grand Canal has a deeper and more profound historical and

段的标志性工程遗址既有以洛阳回洛仓、巩义洛口仓、浚县黎阳仓等为代表的仓储遗址,也有洛阳天津桥、郑州惠济桥、开封州桥、新乡合河石桥、浚县云溪桥这样有代表性的桥梁工程,还有像洛阳南关码头、郑州荥泽枢纽漕运码头、商丘南关汴河码头等标志性码头以及古河堤、古水柜、古水门等遗存遗迹。

其中,回洛仓粮食储量约两亿公斤,是目前中国考古发现仓窖数量最多的隋代"皇家粮仓",充分印证了大运河强大的军事和经济功能。在通济渠商丘南关段,考古人员曾清理出大量建筑砖、瓦,出土的青瓷、白瓷、黑瓷等陶瓷器来自全国各个窑口。这表明唐宋时期宋城南汴河两岸建筑密集,全国各地的大量物资在此集散。与此同时,洛阳隋唐大运河博物馆、开封的小笼包、郑州的贾鲁河、商丘的火神台庙会、滑县的道口烧鸡、浚县的泥咕咕等是具有中原韵味的"千年运河"名片,是传承运河文化、弘扬运河精神、讲述运河故事的重要资源。

浚县的泥咕咕

Nigugu in Xunxian County

cultural value. In the long history, the multiple diversions and frequent flooding of the Yellow River have caused most sections of the Sui-Tang Grand Canal to be submerged in dust. Even at a depth of six or seven meters underground in the old course of the Yellow River, some cultural relics of the Sui-Tang Grand Canal can still be found in many places. According to statistics, there are 10 world cultural heritage sites, 113 national key cultural relic protection units, and 325 provincial cultural relic protection units in the core areas of 40 counties (cities, districts) where the Grand Canal flows through. The landmark engineering sites in Henan section of the Grand Canal include storage sites represented by Huiluo Granary in Luoyang, Luokou Granary in Gongyi, Liyang Granary in Xunxian County, bridge projects represented by Tianjin Bridge in Luoyang, Huiji Bridge in Zhengzhou, Kaifeng Ancient Bridge, Hehe Stone Bridge in Xinxiang and Yunxi Bridge in Xunxian County, historic docks such as Nanguan Wharf in Luoyang, Xingze Hub Wharf in Zhengzhou, Nanguan Bianhe Wharf in Shangqiu, as well as other ancient river banks, water tanks and water gates.

Among these historical sites, Huiluo Granary had a grain reserve of about 200 million kilograms with the largest number of silos found in Chinese archaeological history and was the royal granary of the Sui Dynasty, which fully proved the powerful military and economic functions of the Grand Canal. In the Shangqiu Nanguan section of the Tongji Channel, archaeologists excavated and cleared a large number of building bricks and tiles. There, the unearthed celadon, white porcelain, black porcelain and other ceramics came from various kilns in China. This shows that there were numerous buildings on both sides of the Bianhe River to the south of Songcheng (now Kaifeng City) during the Tang and Song dynasties and a large number of commodities from all over the country were distributed here. Luoyang Sui-Tang Grand Canal Museum, Kaifeng Small Steamed Bun, Zhengzhou Jialu River, Shangqiu Huoshentai Temple Fair, Huaxian County Daokou Roast Chicken and Xunxian County Nigugu are the business cards of the Grand Canal with the characteristics of the Central Plains and the important resources for inheriting the Canal culture, carrying forward the Canal spirit and telling the story of the Canal.

1. 洛阳隋唐大运河博物馆

洛阳隋唐大运河博物馆坐落在河南洛阳老城区，东傍瀍河，南临洛河，西临凤化街，北隔九都路与八路军办事处相对，是全面展示洛阳与大运河的关系及隋唐大运河在洛阳段所遗存的文化遗产的专题性博物馆。

洛阳隋唐大运河博物馆依托全国重点文物保护单位——古建筑群山陕会馆筹建而成，占地面积5000余平方米，建筑面积近3000平方米。现存的洛阳山陕会馆始建于清朝康熙、雍正年间，由当时山西、陕西两地巨商大贾筹资建设。会馆建筑整体为中国传统的中轴线对称分布式两进四合院，主要建筑坐落在中轴线上，次要建筑分落左右，琉璃照壁、西门楼、东西仪门、山门、舞楼围合成第一进院落，舞楼、东西廊坊、东西官厅、拜殿、正殿、东西配殿等围合成第二进院落。

洛阳隋唐大运河博物馆东展厅主要展示隋唐大运河的开凿和隋唐大运河的繁荣和作用。其中就介绍了仁寿四年（604年）七月隋炀帝杨广登基后，于洛阳营建新都，同时为巩固洛阳的政治、军事、经济中心地位，加强对关（山）东、东南地区的控制，确保江南漕粮运抵洛阳，历时六年完成了历史上第一次以洛阳为中心北到北京、南到杭州全长2700公里的南北人工运河，沟通海河、黄河、淮河、长江、钱塘江五大水系，辐射东北、东南，实现了在广大国土范围内南北资源和物产的大跨度调配，促进了不同地域间的经济、文化交流，在国家统一、政权稳定、经济繁荣、文化交流和科技发展等方面发挥了重要作用，促进了以洛阳为代表的运河沿线地区的经济和社会的繁荣发展。

洛阳隋唐大运河博物馆西展厅主要展出了隋唐大运河在洛阳段遗留下来的文化遗迹。宋代以后洛阳逐渐失去了中国政治中心的地位，隋唐大运河洛阳段也逐渐衰落，尤其是元代后运河裁直成为京杭大运河。虽然隋唐大运河不少地方被废弃，但是通济渠（即洛河）仍然发挥着航运作用，对于洛阳的经济和商业保障功不可没，并且一直使用到20世纪

1. Luoyang Sui-Tang Grand Canal Museum

Luoyang Sui-Tang Grand Canal Museum is located in the old city area of Luoyang, Henan Province, bordering the Chan River in the east, the Luohe River in the south, Fenghua Street in the west, and Jiudu Road in the north. It is a special museum that comprehensively displays the relationship between Luoyang and the Grand Canal and the cultural heritage left by the Sui-Tang Grand Canal in Luoyang.

Luoyang Sui-Tang Grand Canal Museum, built on the basis of the ancient buildings of Shanshan Guild Hall, a national key cultural relics protection unit, covers an area of more than 5,000 square meters, including nearly 3,000 square meters of a construction area. The existing Luoyang Shanshan Guild Hall was built during the reign of Emperor Kangxi and Yongzheng in the Qing Dynasty, which was financed by wealthy businessmen of Shanxi and Shaanxi at that time. The whole building of the Shanshan Guild Hall is a Chinese traditional symmetrical two-entry courtyard house with the main building located on the central axis and the secondary buildings on the left and right sides. The glazed glass wall, the west gatehouse, the east and west side gates, the mountain gate, and the dancing house form the first courtyard, while the dancing house, the east and west porches, the east and west official halls, the worship hall, the main hall and the east and west side halls form the second courtyard.

The construction process, prosperity and function of the Sui-Tang Grand Canal is mainly displayed in the east exhibition hall of Luoyang Sui-Tang Grand Canal Museum. In July of the fourth year of Renshou (604), after ascending the throne, Emperor Yang of Sui ordered to build a new capital in Luoyang. At the same time, in order to maintain Luoyang's position as a political, military and economic center, he strengthened his control over the Guandong (Shandong) and the southeast region, so as to ensure that the grain from the south of the Yangtze River could reach Luoyang by water transportation. In this way, the first 2,700-kilometer north-south artificial canal was completed in six years. With Luoyang as the center, the Canal extended from Beijing in the north to Hangzhou in the south, connecting the Haihe River, the Yellow River, the Huaihe River, the Yangtze River and the Qiantang River and radiating to the northeast and southeast regions. After the completion of the Canal, the large-span

中叶。隋唐大运河的遗存历经沧桑也保留了下来，比如通济渠、含嘉仓、回洛仓、天津桥等，让人们管窥昔日运河的风采。

洛阳隋唐大运河博物馆照壁
The screen wall of the Museum of Sui & Tang Grand Canal

洛阳隋唐大运河博物馆是全方位、多角度展现大运河中枢自然特性、人文精华的专题性博物馆。它既是运河文物、文献资料征集、收藏和运河文化研究、展示的中心，也是传播中国运河文化的重要窗口。

2. 巩义洛口仓

洛口仓是世界文化遗产中国大运河标志性工程遗址，是隋唐大运河沿线的重要漕运仓储，对于京城供给、军事需求、灾荒赈济起到了重要作用。洛口仓也叫兴洛仓，位于今河南省郑州市巩义河洛镇七里铺村以东的黄土岭上。这里地处丘陵，形势险要，土层坚硬、干燥，又有水路

allocation of resources and products between the north and the south in the vast territory was realized, and the economic and cultural exchanges between different regions were promoted. The Sui-Tang Grand Canal played an important role in national unification, political stability, economic prosperity, cultural exchanges and scientific and technological development, and brought about the economic and social development and prosperity of the areas along the Canal represented by Luoyang.

The cultural relics of Luoyang section of the Sui-Tang Grand Canal are mainly displayed in the west exhibition hall of Luoyang Sui-Tang Grand Canal Museum. After the Song Dynasty, Luoyang gradually lost its position as the political center of China, and the Luoyang section of the Sui-Tang Grand Canal gradually declined. After the Yuan Dynasty, the Canal was straightened and became the Beijing-Hangzhou Grand Channel. Although many places of the Sui-Tang Grand Canal were abandoned, the Tongji Channel (i.e., Luohe River) still gave full play to the role of shipping, which contributed to the commercial prosperity of Luoyang. So, the Tongji Channel was used until the middle of the twentieth century. The historical remains of the Sui and Tang dynasties, such as the Tongji Channel, Hanjia Granary, Huiluo Granary and Tianjin Bridge, have survived many vicissitudes and given people a glimpse of the Grand Channel in the past.

Luoyang Sui-Tang Grand Canal Museum is a special museum that shows the natural characteristics and humanistic essence of the Grand Canal from all directions and angles. It is not only the center of collecting and enshrining Canal cultural relics and documents as well as the center of Canal cultural research and exhibition, but also the important window of spreading Chinese Canal culture.

2. Luokou Granary in Gongyi

Luokou Granary is the landmark project site of the Grand Canal in China, one of the world cultural heritages. It is an important grain storage for water transport along the Sui-Tang Grand Canal, playing important roles in the capital supply, military demand and famine relief. Luokou Granary, also known as Xingluo Granary, is located on the Huangtu Ridge, east of Qilipu Village, Heluo in Gongyi, Zhengzhou City, Henan Province. It is a hilly and dangerous place,

运输之便。自洛河逆水而上可达当时的首都东都洛阳，逆黄河而上可达陕西潼关和当时的西京长安，顺水而下可达山东至海口，同时与大运河相通，还能南到江苏、浙江，北到河北等省。

605 年，隋炀帝即位不久，就下令建都洛阳，同时下令开凿大运河。大运河以洛阳为起点，经洛河入黄河，然后分两路开凿，向南终点为余杭（今浙江杭州），向北终点为涿州（今北京）。洛口曾是洛河、黄河交汇之处，因大运河的兴修，洛口就坐落在了大运河最为重要的三岔路口上。在大运河新兴的庞大水运网中，洛口具有了举足轻重的地位。隋大业二年（606 年），在巩县东南兴建洛口仓，仓城周围 20 余里，共有 3000 仓窖，每窖藏粮 8000 石，设官兵千人防守粮仓。据此计算，洛口仓约可容纳粮食 2400 万石，是当时全国最大的粮仓，也是大运河最大、最重要的物流中心。这样规模的粮仓，不是为了供应当地消费，甚至也不是为百里之外的首都洛阳储备的，因为洛阳附近另有回洛仓、河阳仓两座大粮仓。显然，大运河的设计者在三岔口摆上这么一座超级大粮仓，是要让其作为调剂东西南北的物流中心。洛口仓兴建后，原本位居四大粮仓之一的河阳仓逐渐失去价值，在隋朝末年已被废弃。

隋代把从江南经大运河运来的粮食囤积于洛口仓。这里粮食物资向西可运往洛阳、长安，渡黄河，经永济渠而运往东北。洛口仓可以说既是东都洛阳的外围粮仓，又是用兵东北的军粮转运站，在隋地位极为重要。

洛口仓曾转运河北、山东以及江淮与江南漕粮，曾为隋唐漕运最大规模仓储群，对东都洛阳的供给、战略物资的储备、灾荒赈济起到了巨大作用，是当时国家富强、府库充裕的保障。与此同时，在隋末的战乱中，洛口仓因存粮丰富，成了各方势力争夺的焦点，大量战争在这里发生，长期的拉锯战也使仓储遭到了严重破坏。瓦岗军李密向首领翟让献计说，洛口仓粮食数量巨大，如果瓦岗军号召天下英雄就仓用粮，天下的各路起义领袖一定响应瓦岗军，听命于翟让，然后翟让就可以称帝号，

with hard and dry soil, but convenient for water transport. Sailing up the Luohe River, people could reach Luoyang, the eastern capital of that time. Upstream to the Yellow River, people were able to arrive in Tongguan and Chang'an (now Xi'an City), the capital. While down the river, people could get to Shandong Province, finally down straight to the mouth of the Yellow River. Meanwhile, the Luohe River is connected to the Grand Canal, with the convenience of getting to Jiangsu and Zhejiang Provinces in the south and Hebei Province in the north.

Soon after Emperor Yang of Sui ascended the throne in 605 AD, he ordered Luoyang to be the capital and people to build the Grand Canal. With Luoyang as the starting point, the Grand Canal passed through the Luohe River into the Yellow River, then it was dug in two ways, ending at Yuhang in the south and Zhuozhou (now Beijing) in the north. Luokou was the junction of the Luohe River and the Yellow River, and due to the construction of the Grand Canal, Luokou was located at the most important divergence of it, playing a pivotal role in the emerging huge water transport network of the Sui-Tang Grand Canal. In the second year of Daye in the Sui Dynasty (606 AD), Luokou Granary was built in the southeast of Gongxian County. About 20 miles around the granary, there were 3,000 cellars, each of which could store 8 thousand dan of grain, being defended by thousands of soldiers. According to the calculation, Luokou Granary could accommodate about 24 million dan of grain, which was the largest granary in China at that time, and the largest and most important logistics center of the Grand Canal. Such a granary of this size was certainly neither for local consumption, nor even for storing grain for Luoyang, the capital a hundred miles away from here, because there were another two large granaries, Huiluo Granary and Heyang Granary near Luoyang. It is clear that the Grand Canal was designed to serve as a logistics hub of the whole country by placing such a huge granary in the divergence. After the construction of Luokou Granary, the Heyang Granary, one of the four granaries, gradually lost its value and was abandoned at the end of the Sui Dynasty.

In the Sui Dynasty, grain was transported from the south of the Yangtze River via Grand Canal and hoarded in Luokou Granary. Food supplies were able to be transported westward to Luoyang and Chang'an, and be shipped to the northeast of China across the Yellow River through the Yongji Channel.

平定中原。这说明得洛口仓就能称帝,失之便会丧邦。大业十二年(616年),翟让和李密的瓦岗军打到荥阳,接近了洛口仓。这时,李密分析了形势,认为百姓饥馑,洛口仓储藏的粮食数量巨大,又容易攻取,因此他建议翟让要不失时机地夺取。翟让采纳了李密的意见,立即派精兵七千,袭击洛口仓,大业十三年(617年),终于攻克洛口仓。瓦岗军占领洛口仓后,立即开仓放粮,赈济饥民,瓦岗军的队伍也得到迅速发展,短时间内猛增至几十万人。李密又令增筑兴洛城,周围四十里,使洛口仓扩大了几倍。瓦岗军在这里建立了农民政权,李密自立为魏公。唐代开元二十一年(733年),重新设置了洛口仓。

中国古代粮仓模型
The model of the granary of ancient China

沧海桑田,时光匆匆,当年的洛口仓已成为历史文化遗迹。但在巩义七里铺村的北岭上,尚存留着长100多米、宽10余米的隋唐城墙,这就是隋唐洛口仓的遗址。在活化运河文化的过程中,结合国家正在河南实施国家粮食生产核心区战略,河南省正在隋唐洛口仓的遗址上建立

Luokou Granary was extremely important in the Sui Dynasty, not only for being the peripheral granary of Luoyang, but also the military grain transfer station of northeast China.

Luokou Granary, as the water transport hub of the Sui-Tang Grand Canal, once transported grain from Hebei, Shandong, Jianghuai (between the Yangtze River and the Huaihe River) and Jiangnan (the south of the Yangtze River), and served as the largest storage cluster in the Sui and Tang dynasties. It played quite important roles in the grain supply of Luoyang, the reserve of strategic materials and the relief of famine. It guaranteed the prosperity of the country and the abundance of the Treasury. At the same time, during the wars at the end of the Sui Dynasty, Luokou Granary, due to the rich grain reserves, became the focus of various forces. Thus, a large number of wars occurred here, and the prolonged seesaw battle caused serious damage to this granary. Li Mi, from the Wagang troops, offered advice to the chief—Zhai Rang that the amount of grain in Luokou Granary was huge, and if the Wagang troops could call on uprising leaders in the whole country to occupy the granary and distribute the grain, all of them must respond to the Wagang troops and took orders from Zhai Rang, who then could proclaim himself the emperor and pacify the Central Plains. This indicated that the person who could obtain the Luokou Granary could claim to be the king, otherwise his nation would be lost. In the twelfth year of Daye in the Sui Dynasty (616 AD), Zhai Rang and Li Mi led Wagang troops to assault Xingyang, and then they were close to Luokou Granary. At that time, Li Mi analyzed the situation that the people were suffering from famine, while the storage of grain in Luokou Granary was large and easy to capture. Therefore, he advised that Zhai Rang should lose no time to seize this opportunity. Zhai Rang accepted Li Mi's advice, and immediately sent seven thousand picked soldiers to attack Luokou Granary. In the next year (617 AD), they finally conquered this granary. Hardly had the Wagang troops occupied the Luokou Granary when they opened the warehouse and distributed grain to relive the famine. So, the Wagang troops were also further strengthened, soaring to hundreds of thousands in a short period of time. Li Mi ordered to expand the Xingluo to 20 kilometers around, several times bigger than before. Wagang troops established a peasant regime there, and Li Mi crowned himself as Wei Gong (a title for the Feudatory King). Luokou Granary

中国古代粮仓博物馆，以再现当时全国最大的粮仓风貌。

3. 商丘火神台庙会

火神台庙会是商丘最为古老和盛大的庙会，被称为"台会"，又称"朝台"，是由人们对祖先阏伯（火神）的祭祀演变成的盛大庙会。

商丘朝拜火神的习俗源自于上古时期，相传阏伯名契，是五帝其中的帝喾之子、帝尧的异母兄，他也是商族部落的始祖、商朝开国君主成汤的先祖。据史料记载，阏伯与兄弟实沈曾居于深林之中，因二人不和，

阏伯台
E Bo Tai

was reset in the twenty-first year (733 AD) in Kaiyuan Reign Period of the Tang Dynasty.

Time brings such great changes to the world that Luokou Granary of those years has become the historical and cultural relics. But on the north ridge of Qilipu Village in Gongyi, there are still walls of more than 100 meters long and ten meters wide, which are the ruins of Luokou Granary in the Sui and Tang dynasties. In the process of reactivating canal culture, under the guidance of the national strategy to enhance the core position of Henan grain production, the Ancient Chinese Granary Museum is being established on the site of Luokou Granary in the Sui and Tang dynasties to recreate the largest granary in China at that time.

3. Huoshentai Temple Fair in Shangqiu

Huoshentai Temple Fair, the oldest and largest temple fair in Shangqiu, is known as "Taihui" (an artistic performance during temple fair), or "Chaotai", a grand temple fair evolved from the sacrifices to the ancestor E Bo (the Vulcan).

In Shangqiu, the custom of worshipping Vulcan dates back to the ancient times. It is said that E Bo was the son of Emperor Ku, one of the five emperors in ancient China, and the half-brother of Emperor Yao. He was the ancestor of Shang tribe, and the ancestor of Chengtang, the founding monarch of the Shang Dynasty. According to historical records, E Bo and his brother Shi Shen once lived in the deep forest. However, due to the discord between them, his father Emperor Ku separated the two brothers and let E Bo move to Shangqiu (now Shangqiu City, Henan Province) and Shi Shen to Daxia (now Taiyuan City, Shanxi Province). When Yao proclaimed himself emperor, E Bo was given the official title of Huo Zheng (also named Si Tu, an official position in ancient times, equal to vice prime minister at present), and later he was crowned the King Xie Xuan. Then he was granted the king of the Kingdom of Shang. It is said that during the period when he took the position of Huo Zheng, he invented the Fire-Calendar, and built a platform, named "E Bo Tai", to observe the stars while taking charge of the fire, on the basis of which he measured the natural changes and the harvest of the year, and E Bo made a great contribution to ancient astronomy in China. He dedicated himself to educating people and was deeply

父亲帝喾把阏伯迁居于商丘（今河南省商丘市），让实沈迁居至大夏（今山西省太原市），将兄弟二人分开。到尧称帝后，阏伯被封为火正（司徒），后又被封为契玄王，之后又被赐封建立商国。据说在担任火正期间，阏伯发明了以火纪时的历法，在管火的同时筑造阏伯台观察星辰，以此为依据测定一年的自然变化和年成的好坏，为中国古老的天文学做出了重要贡献。阏伯呕心沥血，教化民众，深受人民的爱戴，故中国民间尊奉他为"火神"。阏伯死后被葬于阏伯台下，由于阏伯的封号为"商"，他的墓冢也被称为"商丘"，这就是今天商丘市的由来。

在神话故事中，阏伯是天上的火神，偷偷将火种藏在身上，带到了人间。由于阏伯投放火种而违犯了天规，天帝把他贬到凡间为民。同时，天帝发了一场大洪水，要淹没人间的火种，惩罚阏伯。地上的洪水像猛兽一样扑向商丘，人们吓得四处逃散。而为了保存火种，阏伯筑起了高台，搭起了遮雨的棚子，又带领人们四处寻找柴草使火能够持续，天上下雨不能把火浇灭，河水泛滥也不能把火浸灭。阏伯终日为火事操劳，火给百姓带来了幸福，生产和生活条件都大大改善。洪水退后，当人们从四面八方赶回来的时候，高台上的火种还在燃烧，而阏伯已饿死在火种旁边。

抛开神话，正是因为阏伯，人们才有了生活中的长久用火，而且在阏伯的精心管理下火灾大大减少了，阏伯还开创了按照火星运行的规律以纪时，指导当时的农业生产和人民的生活，让人民得到了利益。因此，人们感激阏伯，都说他是天上的神仙下凡给百姓造福来了。阏伯死后，人们怀念他的功德，都怀着崇敬的心情，以当时最厚的葬礼把他葬在他生前保存火种和主星辰之祀的高丘上，从此开始了对阏伯的祭祀。

火神阏伯祭祀虽然起源于商丘，却在历史沿革中波及大江南北，影响深远，上至王侯，下至庶民，都尊阏伯为庇护神。尤其到了南宋时，宋高宗颁旨诏封阏伯为"商丘宣明王"，由皇帝直接主持祭祀商丘宣明王的祀典。阏伯成为南宋朝廷最为崇奉的国运神，崇祀活动伴随南宋朝

loved. Therefore, the Chinese people honored him as Vulcan. After his death, he was buried under the platform, and since his title was "Shang", his tomb was called "Shangqiu", which is the origin of Shangqiu City today.

In the Chinese fairy tale, E Bo is the Vulcan in heaven. Since he secretly hid the allspark and brought it to earth, violating the rules of heaven, the Emperor of Heaven demoted him to earth to become a common person. At the same time, the Emperor of Heaven flooded the earth with the intention of drowning the allspark as a punishment for him. The flood rushed towards Shangqiu region like a beast, and the people fled in terror. In order to preserve the fire, E Bo built a high platform, and put up a shed to resist the rain. Then he led people to collect firewood to make the fire sustainable. Finally the fire was kept. E Bo worked all day long for the fire thing, which brought blessings to the people, with the production and living conditions being significantly improved. After the flood, when people came back from far and near, the fire on the platform was still burning, however E Bo had starved to death beside the fire.

Put aside the myth, under E Bo's careful management, the fire disasters were greatly reduced and people got benefits by using fire and time measurement created by E Bo in accordance with the laws of Mars to guide the agricultural production and people's life. Therefore, people were grateful to him, regarding him as a god from heaven who came to the earth to benefit the people. After his death, people cherished his merits, and buried him with reverence and the grandest funeral at that time on the high hill, where he preserved the fire and worshiped the stars. From then the sacrifices to E Bo began.

Although the sacrifice to E Bo originated in Shangqiu, it has spread far and wide throughout history with profound influence. From nobility to common people, all honored him as a patron saint. Especially in the Southern Song Dynasty (1127-1279), Emperor Gaozong awarded him an honorary decree to call E Bo "Shangqiu Xuanming King", and the emperor himself presided the sacrifice to E Bo. He became the most sublime god in the Southern Song Dynasty, with the worship activities throughout the whole dynasty. Nowadays, Huoshentai Temple Fair is held from the first day of the first lunar month to the second day of the second lunar month. With businesses and folk artists assembling at the junction of Henan, Shandong, Jiangsu and Anhui Provinces, millions of people

廷始终。现如今，每年的正月初一至二月初二，豫、鲁、苏、皖四省交界处的数百万民众、商家、民间艺人纷纷涌来，形成了集祭祀先祖、休闲娱乐、旅游购物、观灯赏马、产品展示、物资文化交流为一体的规模庞大的古庙会。庙会设有总会，各地设有分会，朝拜时由分会会首到总会先行报到，然后由总会安排朝拜时间，按次序进行朝拜。火神台庙会祭祀阏伯传承了中华民族祖先以为民造福为己任、人民不忘圣贤功德薪火相传的优秀文化。

flock to this large-scale ancient Temple Fair which offers sacrifices to their ancestors. In addition, it can provide people with opportunities for leisure and entertainment, tourism and shopping, watching lanterns, displaying products, etc. The Temple Fair has a general assembly, and there are branch venues in various places. When going to the temple, the head of the branch venue will report to the general assembly first, and then the general assembly will arrange the time and order of the worship. The Huoshentai Temple Fair has inherited the excellent culture of the ancestors of the Chinese nation, who regard it as their duty to benefit the people, and the culture that people will never forget the merits and virtues of their sages.

结语：走向世界的大运河

大运河是人类在与大自然相处的过程中的智慧结晶，是人类文明的伟大见证。世界上最著名的运河有中国的大运河、意大利的威尼斯运河、德国的基尔运河、埃及的苏伊士运河和巴拿马的巴拿马运河。中国大运河由京杭大运河、隋唐大运河、浙东运河三部分构成，长度是世界运河之首。其中，京杭大运河长度是巴拿马运河的20倍、苏伊士运河的10倍，是世界大运河中开凿最早、线路最长的一条。作为一条人工开凿的长河，中国大运河见证了春秋、隋、唐、宋、元、明、清的历史，为发展南北交通，沟通南北经济、文化和政治统一做出了巨大的贡献。

从世界范围来说，运河是展示国家形象的重要窗口。中国大运河两岸的码头、船闸、桥梁、堤坝等水工设施，运河沿岸的衙署、钞关、粮仓、会馆、庙宇和驿站等相关设施，是中华文明不同时期的历史反映。中国各地的戏曲、曲艺、文学、艺术、美食、园林，与漕运有关的花会、庙会、河灯、舞龙、高跷、号子、民谣、饮食等，也是大运河流淌的文化符号。

中国大运河河南段曾是国家的生命线中重要的环节，维系着封建王朝的兴盛，也浸透着黎民百姓的苦难。中国大运河河南段由繁华转为衰落的过程，可以折射出中华民族的发展史。中国大运河在国家统一、政权稳定、经济繁荣、文化交流和科技发展等方面发挥了不可替代的作用，对中国和世界历史都产生了巨大和深远的影响。中国大运河因洛阳而实现首次贯通，在中国历史发展过程中发挥着举足轻重的作用，它也是连接丝绸之路，促进中西文化交流、经济繁荣的重要途径。其广阔的时空跨度、巨大的成就、深远的影响成为文明的摇篮，对中华文明产生了深远的影响。

中国的邻近国家和地区以及西亚、欧洲、东非各国通过水运派遣使团和商队来到中国，在各沿海港口泊岸，遂即沿运河航行到达京师及各

Summary: The Grand Canal—Open to the World

As one of the world's longest man-made waterways, the Grand Canal in China provides tangible proof of human wisdom, courage and determination. Its length ranks the first among those famous canals, including the Venice Canal of Italy, the Kiel Canal of Germany, the Suez Canal of Egypt and the Panama Canal of Panama. The Beijing-Hangzhou Grand Canal, the earliest and also the most extensive canal in the world, is 10 times as long as the Suez Canal and 20 times as long as the Panama Canal. The Great Canal has a long history, going through the Sui, Tang, Song, Yuan, Ming and Qing dynasties. The Grand Canal, the main transport artery between the north and the south of China, was a support for ensuring the economic prosperity, social stability and national unification over the ages. It also helped the evolution and bloom of Chinese culture by enhancing the communications between the north and the south in ancient China.

Like the other canals, the Grand Canal is a window to display the image of China to the world. Its wharves, ship locks, bridges, levees, dams and other water engineering facilities, the government offices, granaries, guild halls, temples and post stations along the Canal are living records of different historical periods. The traditional Chinese arts and culture nurtured by the Grand Canal, such as traditional Chinese opera, literature, art, food and gardens appeared nationwide. The flower fairs, temple fairs, river lanterns, dragon dances, ballads, and stilts performance along the course of the Grand Canal revealed the unique cultural tradition of canal management via the water transport system.

The Henan section of the Grand Canal was once an important link in the lifeline of China. It played a significant role in maintaining the prosperity of the feudal dynasties, and it was also built on the sweats and sufferings of the common people. Henan section of the Grand Canal, from prosperity to decline, was an epitome of the developmental history of the Chinese nation. The Grand Canal of China has played an irreplaceable role in national unification, political stability, economic prosperity, cultural exchanges, scientific and technological development, and has far-reaching influence on Chinese and world histories. The different channels of the Grand Canal were first connected in Luoyang. It served greatly in

地，进行着频繁的经济文化交流，有的更直接迁居于运河区，这些地区成为内迁各少数民族和外国使者、商人、学问僧、留学生及其他各方人士集中的地区。他们把中国先进的文化带到世界各地，扩大了中国对世界的影响；而国外优秀的文化也传播到中国，不仅更加丰富了运河区域文化的内容，而且促进了中华民族文化的全面发展。

面对世界百年未有之大变局，面对中华民族伟大复兴历史征程，大运河建设需向世界展示中国和平发展、携手共进的大国形象，展示中国海纳百川的文化胸怀与包容开放的文化信念，展示中国致力构建世界人类命运共同体的大国担当和责任。

building links with the Silk Road, promoting prosperity and cultural exchanges between China and the West. The long-lasting history, great achievements and far-reaching influence of the Grand Canal have nurtured the Chinese civilization.

China's neighboring countries, regions and those in Western Asia, Europe and East Africa, sent envoys and caravans to China by water. They berthed in the coastal ports, and then sailed along the Canal to reach the capital and other places. They had frequent economic and cultural exchanges. Some of them settled down in the Canal areas, where a large number of the envoys, businessmen, learned monks, students and people of different professions, ethnic groups and countries were seen. They spread Chinese culture to the other parts of the world, and brought the diverse foreign cultures into China, which not only enriched the regional Canal culture, but also promoted the national Chinese culture.

In face of the unprecedented international changes over a century and in face of the rejuvenation of the nation, China hopes to show the world, through the reconstruction of the Grand Canal and rediscovery of its culture, that it is a nation that has shouldered and will continue to shoulder its responsibilities as a member of the world, a nation committed to peace and joint development, a nation that shows great concerns about the shared future for mankind in the world, and a nation whose culture is rooted in tolerance, inclusiveness and opening.

附录：中国历史年代简表
Appendix: A Brief Chronology of Chinese History

中国历史年代简表
A Brief Chronology of Chinese History

五帝时代 Period of the Five Legendary Rulers c. 2600 BC–c. 2070 BC	黄帝 Huangdi (Yellow Emperor)	
	颛顼 Zhuanxu	
	帝喾 Diku (Emperor Ku)	
	尧 Yao	
	舜 Shun	
夏 Xia Dynasty	c. 2070 BC–c. 1600 BC	
商 Shang Dynasty	c. 1600 BC–c. 1046 BC	
西周 Western Zhou Dynasty	c. 1046 BC–c. 771 BC	
东周 Eastern Zhou Dynasty 770 BC–256 BC	春秋 Spring and Autumn Period	770 BC–476 BC
	战国 Warring States Period	475 BC–221 BC
秦 Qin Dynasty	221 BC–206 BC	
汉 Han Dynasty 206 BC–220 AD	西汉 Western Han	206 BC–25 AD
	东汉 Eastern Han	25 AD–220 AD
三国 Three Kingdoms 220 AD–280 AD	魏 Wei	220 AD–265 AD
	蜀汉 Shu Han	221 AD–263 AD
	吴 Wu	222 AD–280 AD
晋 Jin Dynasty 265 AD–420 AD	西晋 Western Jin	265 AD–317 AD
	东晋 Eastern Jin	317 AD–420 AD

续表 Continued Table

南北朝 Southern and Northern Dynasties 420 AD-589 AD	南朝 Southern Dynasties	宋 Song	420 AD-479 AD
		齐 Qi	479 AD-502 AD
		梁 Liang	502 AD-557 AD
		陈 Chen	557 AD-589 AD
	北朝 Northern Dynasties	北魏 Northern Wei	386 AD-534 AD
		东魏 Eastern Wei	534 AD-550 AD
		北齐 Northern Qi	550 AD-577 AD
		西魏 Western Wei	535 AD-556 AD
		北周 Northern Zhou	557 AD-581 AD
隋 Sui Dynasty		581 AD-618 AD	
唐 Tang Dynasty		618 AD-907 AD	
五代十国 Five Dynasties and Ten States	五代 Five Dynasties 907 AD-960 AD	后梁 Later Liang	907 AD-923 AD
		后唐 Later Tang	923 AD-936 AD
		后晋 Later Jin	936 AD-947 AD
		后汉 Later Han	947 AD-950 AD
		后周 Later Zhou	951 AD-960 AD
	十国 Ten States 902 AD-979 AD	北汉 Northern Han	951 AD-979 AD
		吴 Wu	902 AD-937 AD
		吴越 Wuyue	907 AD-978 AD
		闽 Min	909 AD-945 AD
		南汉 Southern Han	917 AD-971 AD
		荆南(又称"南平") Jingnan (Nanping)	924 AD-963 AD
		楚 Chu	927 AD-951 AD
		南唐 Southern Tang	937 AD-975 AD
		前蜀 Former Shu	907 AD-925 AD
		后蜀 Later Shu	934 AD-965 AD

续表 Continued Table

宋 Song Dynasty 960 AD-1279 AD	北宋 Northern Song	960 AD-1127 AD
	南宋 Southern Song	1127 AD-1279 AD
辽 Liao (契丹 Qidan/Khitan)	907 AD-1125 AD	
西夏 Xixia (Tangut)	1038 AD-1227 AD	
金 Jin	1115 AD-1234 AD	
元 Yuan Dynasty	1206 AD-1368 AD	
明 Ming Dynasty	1368 AD-1644 AD	
清 Qing Dynasty	1616 AD-1911 AD	
中华民国 Republic of China	1912 AD-1949 AD	
中华人民共和国 People's Republic of China	1949 AD-	